Dedication:

To Dave who picks me up before I even realize I'm down.

To Kayla and Hanalei who inspire me to live a big, delicious life.

And to my loving and supportive family, especially my moms and dad, without whom I wouldn't be here.

For my many clients who keep me growing just to stay one step ahead of them.

CONTENTS

INTRODUCTION .... 1.

HOW TO USE THIS BOOK .... 7.

1. The Two-Minute Meditation Method: .... 9.
Short-Burst Meditation, Just Once a Day

2. Your Body Is More Than Just a Body: .... 17.
Your Body is Your Best Source of Information

3. Don't Just Practice Self-Care: Master the .... 25.
Art of Treasuring Yourself

4. Big Feelings Are a Gift, Not a Curse: .... 31.
This is For All of You Who Were Ever Told,
"You Are Too Much!"

5. Loving Your Broken Places: How to .... 39.
Shift From Perfect and Disconnected, to
Authentic and Deeply Connected

6. Clean Out Your Underwear Drawer: You .... 43.
Deserve Only the Best Underwear

7. Nature Hates a Vacuum: How to Use .... 51.
This Truth to Your Advantage

8. You May Be Missing the Full Power .... 57.
of This Gratitude Thing: Just One
Little Change and The Power Will Be
Unleashed!

9. The Secret of Affirmations .... 61.

10. The Magic of Wanting a Cup of Coffee: .... 65.
The Subtle Art of Wanting What You Want

11. Reality is What You Make Of It: Pay Attention to What You Want More Of .... 69.

12. Let's Play the "What If" Game .... 79.

13. Three Powerful Little Words: The Key to Navigating the Most Difficult Situations .... 83.

14. Whomever or Whatever is Most Unlovable, Needs the Most Love .... 89.

15. Grow Some Boundaries .... 93.

16. A New Way of Thinking About Attention Deficit Disorder (It May Not be What You Think) .... 97.

17. Deep Listening Like Medicine for the Soul .... 103.

18. Practice Good Mental Health .... 109.

19. Give Yourself Some Grace and Space .... 113.

20. A Simple Meditation .... 117.

21. How To Make Peace With Trauma .... 123.

22. What You Say s What You Get: Your Words are More Powerful Than You Think .... 127.

23. To Receive is Just as Blessed as to Give: Rewriting an Old, Unhealthy Script .... 131.

24. Ask and You Shall Receive: How to Reverse Engineer Your Life .... 135.

25. The Power Hidden in Just Breathing .... 141.

CONCLUSION .... 147.

Even Small Changes Can Yield Profound Results

We all do it—get caught up in the idea that *everything* has to change for a truly meaningful impact. New Year's Resolutions, total diet overhauls, ending important relationships, moving to a new place, changing careers. Sure, these large-scale changes definitely create large-scale shifts. But we have forgotten the power of shifting just a little something. We have neglected a much simpler and often sweeter way to effect change: Just change *something—anything*, even something tiny—and big changes inevitably occur.

This way of changing things is grounded not just in my personal experience or experience with my clients, or even anecdotal evidence from hundreds of years across every culture, although it certainly is all of that. It is also firmly rooted in scientific study. The Butterfly Effect, born out of chaos theory, was the brainchild of meteorologist, Edward Lorenz. His seminal paper was entitled, "Does the Flap of a Butterfly's Wings in Brazil Set Off a Tornado in Texas?" And his answer was a resounding "YES!"

The simple truth behind this theory is that everything is so intricately intertwined that even a minute event (like the flap of a butterfly wing), completely changes the trajectory of events from there on out.

I feel this truth as I move through my everyday life. This is definitely in my mind when I am faced with a major decision. But it is also in my mind as I choose what to feed my family, as I meet with a client, as I get my overarching goal in mind before having a difficult conversation. Each of these small moments in time also set in motion a cascade that culminates in a much larger impact.

There is a visual image that helps me keep this concept in mind and I want to share it with you. It goes like this:

There is a little group of feathers on all birds of prey that functions sort of like our thumbs. It is called the Alula. Although the feathers and the overall structure of the Alula are small, the function is not. This tiny grouping of feathers can be moved by just a millimeter and the heavy bird's entire trajectory will change. One of the more spectacular examples of this is when the bird is hovering, high in the air, honing-in on its prey and preparing to dive bomb for the kill. The Alula of an eagle, for instance, enhances the drop speed and fine-tunes the attack zone from up to 100 stories high by making just the tiniest adjustment.

For the raptor, this can be the difference between feast or famine—between life or death. For us, the lesson of the Alula may not always be life or death. But it is still hugely impactful.

The lesson is simple and clear: You don't have to make a huge change to receive massive results.

I have had the joy of learning this lesson (along with so many others) over and over in my twenty years of working with pregnant and birthing individuals, parents, newborns, the elderly, and thousands of other clients. I started this journey at four years old when my own mother died. The lessons were intense and life changing: Loss is devastating; I am stronger than anyone could have imagined; people say really stupid things with the best of intentions; people can look like they have the best of intentions, but actually don't; people are almost always more scared and broken than they seem; I have the power to choose how I want to feel about difficult situations; even when it feels like I absolutely am I absolutely am not alone.

The lessons continued as I got older. I read everything I could get my hands on from world religions to quantum physics, from Parent Effectiveness Training to medical journals. Working as a freelancer for a few days or weeks at over a hundred different companies in New York City was an education in human nature that could not have been richer. Helping my father complete his doctorate in psychology was a great vicarious education, and medical massage school provided the rest of the foundation upon which I developed a deep understanding of how the mind and body and spirit work together.

I stepped into birth work after giving birth to our first daughter. There are few experiences in life that require you to bring forward 100% of the best of you in a magical mix of body, mind, spirit, and emotions like giving birth does and I was hooked. I wanted to help others experience this power. First as a doula, then as a midwife, then teaching others how to be midwives and doulas, the intricacies and intimacy of birth have taught me so much about the intricacies of being human.

Now my day-to-day life is made up of teaching, sessions with private clients for intuitive bodywork, spiritual guidance, life coaching, Somatoemotional Release and trauma resolution, and attending births. I find myself reaching for the same tools over and over as I work with people—tools I've developed in the wee hours of the morning at a fifty-hour birth, tools I've developed in response to a newborn who has come through a traumatic birth, tools I've discovered by practicing deep listening to countless stories from countless people in the quiet of my office.

My favorites of these tools are in this book, and this book is my gift to you. I hope you find yourself reaching for these tools just as I do—throughout any normal day, but especially when life becomes overwhelming or difficult, or when you feel the need to shift something.

I have learned that if you don't have good tools readily available to you, you will reach for the old ones. Sure, you will still make it through one way or another, but you will inevitably find yourself stuck in the same old patterns, using the same old tools that keep you recreating the exact life you *don't* want. By just getting through, you miss the deeper opportunity to blow through the "getting through" and emerge into the "glorious." Surviving is not the same as thriving. And thriving is what I wish for you.

Notes: _____

HOW TO USE THIS BOOK

You can read the whole book and just soak everything in. This is a good option with positive impact.

You can read each chapter, but don't *just* read it—actually practice using the tool in each chapter. This is a great option with much more impact. When you work with the tools, you truly integrate them—you own them and will find yourself reaching for them when you are stressed or overwhelmed.

You can read each chapter with a friend, a book club, or other small group of supportive people. Having the support and accountability of another person or small group of people can amplify and deepen the experience of working with this book.

You can open the book anywhere and start reading, letting intuition guide you to the correct place for what you need in your life at that moment. My Grandma Ima taught me to do this. She was a deeply religious woman, so she used the Bible for this and called it "Bible Dipping." But she believed it could be done with any book if you prayerfully held a question in your head and asked for guidance. You can apply this same technique using this book by asking a question or saying a prayer for guidance, closing your eyes, and just opening the book as the spirit moves you. The first passage your eyes land on when you open them is your response.

Whichever way you use this book, whether on your own or with a friend or small group, I'm so glad you have it in your hands. Each chapter offers you a powerful tool that has the potential to help you identify and move out of stuck places, allowing you to breathe into bigger dreams that can grow into the richest, most delicious life you can possibly imagine.

CHAPTER 1

The Two-Minute Meditation Method: Short-Burst Meditation, Just Once a Day

This is your first tool because it is the quickest way to get the biggest return on investment. Just two tiny minutes a day will lay a solid foundation for big shifts.

It seems like everyone these days is talking about how meditation is good for practically everything. It is suggested as an aid for pretty much anything from migraines to stress; poor digestion to high blood pressure.

In my own life, I have seen profound benefits including deeper sleep, less extreme reactions to stressful situations at work and home, and the ability to maintain a sense of faith and peace. The level of stress in my life definitely has not changed, but as I have settled into the practice of just *two minutes of meditation each day,* the stress does not impact me in the same way because I am so much more grounded.

Okay. Wait. What the heck does *grounded* even mean? There is a lot of talk about being grounded—about how we need to be more grounded—but no one explains what it *really* means. And also, how do you even do it?

Grounded means you are not in a reactive state 24/7. It means that you approach life from a place of peace and belief that *all is well* even if it doesn't seem like it, rather than responding to any stimuli like everything is careening off the rails and we're all gonna die a fiery death!

What it means on a physiological level is that you have reset your nervous system. You are settled down out of fight-or-flight mode where-in your body pumps a steady stream of stress hormones like adrenaline and cortisol. You are now in a calmer, less reactive state. (If you've heard of "adrenal fatigue," this constant fight-or-flight state is what leads to it.)

From this place of calm you have the ability to: see things more clearly; respond with more kindness and intention; vastly reduce the amount of anxiety and worry you experience; and enjoy the peace that comes from looking down on the forest rather than getting tangled up in the underbrush.

I've heard all the excuses for not meditating—most of them from myself.

"I can't sit still."

"But my mind never gets quiet."

"Meditation makes me more anxious because I'm afraid I don't do it right."

Valid concerns. But I'm going to tell you all of the secrets to becoming a meditation master today. Right now!

1. You don't have to sit still. Try a moving meditation.
Do some dishes as you let your mind relax. Or go for a two-minute walk outside. The only reason to have your phone with you is to set a timer. Let's play a game: Focus on your breath, and each time you notice your mind catching on a thought, just bring your mind back to your breath until the end of the block. Then, for the next block, do the same thing. Do this for two minutes—just gently bring your mind back to your breath. That's it. You just meditated!

2. You don't have to make your mind quiet. No one ever truly stops the stream of thoughts while meditating... That's not even the goal.

My favorite illustration of meditation came from working with a client who grew up on the Niagara River. She practically had river water running through her veins from spending so much time in, around, and on that powerful body of water. So to make my concept of meditation make sense to her on a cellular level, I described it like this:

"You had a long dock out into the river, right? Well, as flotsam and jetsam came down the river, didn't it get caught in the back eddy, swirling there in the corner beside your dock?" She admitted that there was often a loose jumble of debris including the occasional dead fish or bird.

"How did you clear that stuff out of there?" I asked. She described a wide, flat, wooden rake on a long pole that she and her siblings used for this purpose. "We would just push all that stuff out of the eddy and back out into the moving stream of the river," she said, illustrating the movement with her arms and hands.

"That's it!" I said. "That's all you need to meditate: a mental debris rake on a long pole that you use to gently sloosh thoughts out of the corners where they get caught and out into the moving stream so you can just watch them float on by."

So it goes like this: A thought comes down the river: "Oh crud. I forgot to move the laundry from the washer to the dryer." You then think, "Gah. Now all those clothes are probably mildewy and I'll have to run that load again and I won't have time to get it all done before soccer practice. I am so disorganized. I am the worst parent on the planet."

And... boom. You are now caught in that back eddy—just swirling around and around. Stuck in an old pattern of negative thinking. But it's okay. You can't do this wrong. Just pick up your rake and sloosh that pile of thoughts back out into the stream and watch them float on by. Just keep doing that over and over. And over. Aaaaaand over. No judgment. No frustration. No anxiety. Just note the debris and sloosh it back into the stream.

3. And that takes care of the #3 worry about meditation.

There is no need to be anxious that you are doing it wrong because you can't do this wrong. That process of taking a walk and gently returning to your breath, or of doing dishes and just noticing your thoughts as they swirl around with the dishwater, or of getting hung up on the debris and then moving it back out into the stream IS meditating.

Now do this for just two minutes each day. That's all you get. You're not allowed to do more.

This little practice teaches you how to watch your thoughts float by without attaching stories or emotions to them. It gently entrenches the idea that:

> You are not your thoughts.
> You are the river.

But that's not all, friends. You get a super-special, amazing gift with purchase! This is the ultimate BOGO offer!

The other powerful thing you get when you do this for *just two minutes a day* is that you can now say with complete truthfulness, "I am a meditator." "I meditate."

Yeah, okay. It's only for two minutes a day. But that doesn't change the fact that you do it! Therefore, you are a meditator.

You meditate.

When you commit to just those two minutes each day and do it, you are not just going to reap all the amazing benefits of consistent meditation. You will, of course. But you are also changing how you feel about yourself. Think of how you feel about that friend who is always there for you. Who you can count on to follow through with what she said she would do even when the you-know-what is hitting the fan. You can relax with her, right? You don't have to second-guess her motives or be afraid that you will be left holding the bag.

It's the same with yourself. All those times you said you were going to do something . . . and then didn't. All the ways you have undermined your best intentions. All the times you needed strength and acceptance and love the most and you didn't show up for yourself. That is going to change now. Because you are going to do this one thing every. single. day. It's only two minutes. That's it. Just two minutes.

When you do this every single day for just two minutes, you are quite literally changing yourself on the physiological level—you are remapping the synaptic pathways in your brain. But you are also changing yourself on an energetic level—you are showing up for yourself. Just like a best friend would. You are forging a new trust in yourself. And this trust will ripple positivity out into every corner of your life.

That's a lot of return on investment for just two minutes a day.

1. Make a commitment to yourself that you will totally show up for *just two minutes each and every day.*

2. Meditate for just two minutes each and every day. You can do this while taking a walk, doing dishes, sitting on the toilet seat in the back bathroom while your kids pound on the door... I don't care where or even how you do it. I just care **that** you do it—for just two minutes each and every day.

3. Remember: it's only for two minutes. Set a timer or use my guided Two Minute Meditation Method recording, available at: https://www.aprilkline.com/two-minute-meditation

Your Body Is More Than Just a Body: Your Body is Your Best Source of Information

Many of us have a love/hate relationship with our bodies. We have to take care of them: feed them, sleep them, move them, etc. But, despite this level of care, most of us have gotten really good at not being very in touch with our own bodies. This leaves us feeling disconnected, isolated even. Over time, this can lead to chronic illness, pain, making poor decisions, or not being able to make decisions at all.

"Mind-Body" is a total catch phrase these days. We are told to be mindful, to get out of our heads, to get into our bodies, to do yoga, to love our bodies, to practice self-care. It all sounds great, but how in the world are we supposed to actually do this whole Mind-Body thing?

The interesting thing is that being in touch with your body is not difficult. It's actually pleasant once you get over any initial resistance. Take a minute right now to get in touch with your body. Nothing too serious—just start at your toes and notice how they feel right now. Are they touching the ends of your shoes? Pinched, twisted, relaxed? Are they happy or miserable? If you don't really know, don't think too much about it—just go with the first thought that comes into your head.

Now move up to the tops of your feet. Check in there. How are these parts of your feet feeling right now? Relaxed? Tight? Tired? Just right? Now the arches of your feet. How do these parts of your feet feel right now?

Keep moving up your body and do the same thing with each part—just tune in and really feel that little part. As you leave each area, notice how it connects to the area before it and the area after.

When you reach the top of your head, say a simple, "Thank you," to your body. Thank it for being there for you. That's it. That is the simplest way to practice "Mind-Body" awareness.

Having a body, a mind, emotions, and a spirit is a lot to manage. It is often totally overwhelming. So most of us have been taught that the way to manage it is to disconnect from our bodies so we don't feel so much. But here's the thing: Your body is not just what gets you from point A to point B. It is not just something to feed and water and exercise and have lots of mixed emotions about because it is too big or too little, too fat or too thin, the wrong color, too painful. That's the sad piece of garbage we have swallowed for generations. But it is just not true, and it is time to change that sad story.

We are not just bags of blood and bone. We are also not just souls walking around inside physical containers/bodies. Nor are we a jumble of random emotions. What we actually are is a complex mash-up of all of those things. We are physical/psychological/emotional/spiritual beings.

And your body is actually the key to feeling connected and grounded and happier. It is an oh-so-important part of the physical/psychological/ emotional/spiritual being that you are. And it is definitely your best source of deep information.

Your body is nothing less than the way you gather all the data points around which you build your reality. Your interpretation and, therefore, your reactions and responses to that reality are based 100 percent on information you have gathered through your body and its exquisite senses. Your knowledge—your intuition—are completely grounded in your physical self. It is no mistake that we say, "I had a **gut** feeling," when we are describing just knowing something.

I believe that the "still, small voice" so many of us have heard about is easiest to hear when we listen to our bodies. **This is a life-changing truth.** It leads to making big, wild decisions. It leads to feeling powerful in-and-of-yourself. It causes you to say and do things that are not middle-of-the-road—and that can make others feel very uncomfortable. Largely for this reason, most of us are taught from birth not to listen, not to value, not to trust—even to hate our incredible bodies—the root of all our knowing. Because if you are really connected in your body, you will find you are complete. And if you are complete, you are not looking outside yourself for something else to make you whole. You are not always looking for that next thing that will "make you awesome." Because you are totally rooted in the fact that you are already awesome—in your brittle, broken, supple, crazy, beautiful wholeness.

But we have been taught that our bodies are too painful, too complicated, too much. So we resist hearing that still, small voice whispering to us through our bodies. And one of two things happens: that voice gets louder and more insistent—demanding that we listen. And, if we still resist, it will become even more vehement and our bodies become more painful and even ill over time.

Or, sadly, that still, small whisper gives up. It just goes silent. We all know what that looks like: the hollow expression—the body is there, but no one is home. Everything can look right—even beautiful—on the surface, but there is nothing underneath.

When humans experience something overwhelming or "too big," we typically deal with it by disconnecting to reduce the impact on our systems. This self-protective move can be a lifesaver in the short term, but, over time, it leads to being completely disconnected—to feeling numb and separate from our lives. When we begin to connect back into our bodies, we start to feel again and—BOOM—up comes what has been shoved down. All of it. This can be so scary. It can feel like you are going to get stuck in this emotional quicksand and feel like this forever. But I promise you are not. Take comfort in the fact that you are actually doing exactly what you need to do to move this garbage out of your system.

When you allow this garbage to move—when you take a deep breath and just acknowledge the overload of backed up information you receive from your body in all of its messy, complicated, painful glory, that still, small voice will be able to speak more clearly. **As you simply *acknowledge* the message, rather than reacting and judging, that voice enters into a true dialogue with you and the messages get more manageable and clearer.** You begin to interact with that voice and trust it to inform your ideas about your life. And, as your relationship grows, you will even begin to seek its counsel in your decision-making.

By listening to these messages—these truths from your body— you will actually release stuck places in your physical and metaphysical body. *Doing this literally sets you free.* When you are not stuck, you flow. When you flow, you react effortlessly and appropriately to stimuli. You do not blow all your energy just "reacting" to "over-reacting all the time and, therefore, you will have more energy to do the things you really want to do.

I'm not suggesting this is an easy habit to form. What I am saying without any reservation whatsoever, is that this little habit is a huge key to a happier, more fulfilling life.

PRO TIP: When you begin to really acknowledge what you feel—all of it: the good, the bad, the ugly—without judgment and extreme reaction—you begin to be grateful for your body because it is the exquisite conduit through which you experience your life. When you are rooted in your body, you don't care so much what it looks like, as you care how healthy it is. You want to feed it nourishing food so it can work more efficiently. You want to move it because it feels so good and because it makes your body healthier and, therefore, a better conduit of information. You want to rest it and meditate and pray with it so you can gather even clearer messages through it.

> When you love something, you naturally want to take exquisite care of it.

This becomes a positive feedback loop wherein you take better care of your body because it is feeding you better information, your body gives you clearer and more complete information, you process more of that information, you love your body for feeding you better information, you take better care of your body because it is feeding you better information...

Connect deeply. Connect deeply within your body.

DO THIS:

Two small ways to connect deeply within your body that will give you profound results:

1) I refer you back to Chapter 1 because having a daily practice of meditation or prayer is the number one way to get more deeply in tune with your body. If you practice watching what messages come through your consciousness rather than reacting to those messages, you will start to flow more freely.

Part of this is simply being still. We are very used to a lot of stimuli all. the. time. We look at our phones an average of six to eight hours per day according to Common Sense Media. We have on music, sit in crowded coffee shops, watch shows, travel more than any previous generation... we don't even pump gas without a TV screen in our faces. How could we possibly hear any messages (especially messages that might be difficult, scary, or painful) from our bodies with all of that distraction?

Every world religion offers the simple (but challenging) stricture to "Be still and know." This is good advice. Definitely worth a try for just two minutes a day.

2) The other easy way to get back into your body is to do something lovely with your body. Find something your body really loves to do and make it a priority to do it regularly. Walking, swimming, yoga. My body loves to walk and run on trails in the woods. I feel my breath deepen. I feel my mind flatten and widen out to the horizon. I also often find myself shedding tears as I go deeper into the woods. "Better out than in," I tell myself. "Just feel that feeling. Is it sadness? Loneliness? Fear? Overwhelm? It doesn't even matter. Just feel it." All the while, I'm not stuck in this feeling, because I am literally moving through it as I walk and run. Soon, the feeling dissipates. There's more of a bounce in my step and I'm thinking happier, more hopeful thoughts. All of that emotion has been poured out onto the forgiving forest floor and I can return to my day a whole lot lighter and clearer.

CHAPTER 3

Don't Just Practice Self-Care: Master the Art of Treasuring Yourself

There is so much talk today about self-care. Ideas about what it means to practice self-care. People are beginning to realize that true self-care is more than just getting a facial or a pedicure. There is an emerging conversation about practicing self-care by getting better sleep, clearing out old stuff both internally and externally, even growing stronger boundaries. But, while these are a great place to start, there is a lot more depth available to us than just this.

What if you actually took care of yourself in the same exact way you take care of the thing or person you value more than anything else in this whole world?

Let's say your one thing is your car. All your life, you have settled for okay cars, but this—well, this is the car. You saved up for the down payment, you give up little luxuries every month to make the monthly payment, you keep it in a warm garage, you wash and vacuum it weekly and get it detailed a couple times a year. This car! You would only let people who are responsible and understand the true value of your car anywhere near it. And you enjoy the heck out of it! Nothing beats the feeling of getting behind the wheel of that car, rolling down the windows, cranking up the tunes, and hitting the road. In short, you treasure your car. You take exquisite care of it. And it rewards you by adding immense value to your life.

Let's try something.

1) Name the most valuable thing or person to you in the whole world. (You must pick just one.)

2) Write down all the feelings that stir in your heart when you think about that thing or person.

3) List all the ways you demonstrate your care for this thing or person.

4) List all the ways your life is richer because of this thing or person.

And that's it. Right there. Look at all the things you are willing to do for your beloved thing or person. All the hoops you're willing to jump through, all the scrimping you'll do, all the ferocious protecting you will do, all the benefit of the doubt you'll extend, all the treats and gifts you'll give, all the time you'll share.

Now imagine how it would feel if you did all of that FOR YOU. Imagine how loved you would feel. How much more willing you would be to go above and beyond for yourself if you felt so cared about—so cared for. So treasured.

This is actually a super simple thing to do and will repay you a thousand-fold.

1) Get out the previous exercise and rewrite all the things you do that demonstrate how much you care for your most loved thing or person on a new piece of paper.

2) Tape the paper to your bathroom mirror or put it on your desk next to your keyboard or some other place you look every day.

3) Pick just one of those things and do it for yourself today. Just one. I don't care if it feels forced or silly. Do it anyway.

4) Tell yourself you love yourself so much, you want to do this nice thing to demonstrate how much you care.

5) Really feel how it feels when you do that one thing for yourself.

Your feelings may not be so positive at first. You may find yourself feeling guilty. Guilty about spending the money or taking the time. You may find yourself listing off all the other things you should be doing. You may find yourself feeling weepy or angry. These are all natural reactions to the growing realization that you have lived on the dredges, the leftovers, the scraps for all these years.

Feel those feelings and gently tell yourself, "I understand this feels strange. But I love you and I want you to know it. So I'm going to do this anyway."

You can repeat the same gesture of love the next day, or you can choose one of the other items on your list. As you do this one small thing every day, you are teaching yourself to have faith in you. You are laying an unshakeable foundation of trust that you have your back, that you will go to the mat for yourself, that you love yourself no matter what and that you deserve to be treasured.

This little practice is way more powerful than giving yourself a facial or getting a pedicure. Those are delightful and may well be things you will do for yourself as gestures of care. But they won't do this bedrock level work in and of themselves. What you are doing with this exercise is changing your narrative about yourself—about what you deserve in life. This is where the real shift takes place. This is where you store up extra for when times get tough. This is how you grow courage to try harder things than you ever thought you could try before. This is how you explode into the biggest, most abundant life you can imagine.

> Just show up for yourself in one small way every day, and yourself will explode with joy and love and return your investment a thousand times over.

CHAPTER 4

⁓⁓⁓

Big Feelings Are a Gift, Not a Curse: This is For All of You Who Were Ever Told, "You Are Too Much!"

Have you ever been told, "You're too loud," "You're overwhelming," "You are too much "

These messages are usually fed to us as children by well-meaning adults who are either overwhelmed themselves or are worried about having kids who don't look like "good children" (e.g., quiet, responsive and well-mannered).

When someone tells me they've been talked to like this, I know two things: 1) They are sensitive souls who have not been understood, much less appreciated. They certainly have not been taught how to be a sensitive soul in this overwhelming world. And, 2) They have tried to stuff themselves down for so long—trying to be more palatable—that they've forgotten who they really are. They have played small, bitten back their words, and dumbed themselves down in a sad attempt to be more acceptable. Maybe they seem to fit in a little better, but that smaller self they put out into the world isn't the real them. They feel like what people find acceptable is just a pathetic cardboard cutout stuck in front of the real, gigantic flesh and blood and mind and spirit that they truly are.

When these people step into my office, within minutes, they start to cry. Those are tears of relief because they finally feel safe enough to let that cardboard cutout fall away and let the real person behind it come forward. They usually apologize, but I always say the same thing: "I'm so glad you're crying. That means things are moving! Thank you for being brave enough to be here as your real self."

When we are allowed to really experience our emotions unapologetically and share the experience, several powerful things happen:

1) We strengthen our understanding of who we really are.

2) We create a deeper bond of trust with the person we share with.

3) We encourage others that it is okay to feel their feelings and truly express themselves.

4) We break the bonds of secret shame that lock us into isolation and loneliness—which sets us free.

Imagine how different things would be if you had been told your feelings were valid—really big, perhaps, but also valid. Seriously. Close your eyes for a minute and imagine it like this: You feel completely overwhelmed. You are frustrated to the point where you cannot contain yourself and all that energy has to come out somehow. So, you start yelling, and maybe you pick up a chair and smash it down. Or you leave the room and slam the door behind you so the pictures jump on the wall. And one of your people comes to you and simply sits down near you. Quietly, the person says, "Wow. You are really upset. It seems like you are super frustrated."

How does that feel?

If you are like most people, it feels like someone has just let all the air out of an over-filled balloon. Like you can breathe again. Your heart rate slows. You are able to think again. Then the real work can take place: the work of figuring out how you got into that state in the first place. Is this current stuff or old stuff that never got resolved? Or maybe it's a mixture of the two. You will find that working with the emotions after you have felt really seen and validated is very different from what happens when you have been shamed for not being able to control yourself—when you have felt judged for your "poor behavior." It is much more possible to do the hard work of thinking through how this happened and come up with some ideas that might help it not happen as often when you are not feeling like you are just a horrible problem for everyone—that you are too much and too big to handle.

Let's dissect this idea that your feelings are too much or too big for others to handle. Each time you have felt that way, it has left a scar. Each time. And know this: The times you felt that way very likely go clear back to before you had conscious memory. When you were a tiny baby and cried "too much" or "too long" or "What is wrong with this kid?? All they do is cry," you were being fed the message that you were too much and too big. And then layer upon layer of this message got reinforced throughout your childhood. It began to feel correct. It became an unpleasant belief about yourself. And the saddest thing is that, even though it is unpleasant, it now feels correct and comfortable because it is all you have ever known.

Now, here you are, all these years later, wondering why you feel stuck in this pattern of playing small and then exploding. And not having much of an idea how to break out of it.

The important differentiation here is that **your emotions are not the same thing as your feelings.** We often use them interchangeably, but they are actually very different. *Emotions* are transitory. They are ruled by circumstances and are usually reactionary. Emotions are what come exploding out of us like a hurricane and seem really big and overwhelming to others. *Feelings* are deeper and move slower, like ocean waves. They are ruled by our connection with Spirit and are the foundation of what makes us really us. When we say, "You hurt my *feelings*," what we are really saying is, "That thing you did wounded the deepest part of what makes me *me*."

When we are tiny babies, we are completely ruled by our emotions. They are our only means of experiencing the world and our only way of communicating. Think how frustratingly limited that must feel to our little selves—every need we have for our very *survival* must be communicated with these limited emotional tools. And when our grown-ups are busy, not tuned in, exhausted, worried, distracted, etc., small emotions often don't get the response we need. So, we resort to big emotions to get the attention we require. And then there is a negative response to us and our *big* emotions. And thus the pattern begins.

But, as adults, we have the ability to be very specific about this difference between our *emotions* and our *feelings*. There is power in this differentiation. Our real power comes from being less controlled by our *emotions* and more in tune with our *feelings*.

As you practice your daily two-minute meditation, as you get down into your body more regularly, as you start to shift the internal dialogue, you will become a master of knowing whether what you are experiencing is an *emotion* or a *feeling*.

DO THIS:

1) The next time you feel overwhelmed by an upsurge of anger/ jealousy/fear/ overwhelm/impatience/etc., Practice The Pause. Take one minute to just notice what you're feeling. Feel where you are feeling it in your body. For example: Where is your breath stopping on its way in? This is a huge clue. If it gets stopped in your throat or upper chest, you can be assured you are experiencing an *emotion*.

2) Excuse yourself from the situation. My catch phrase (which my children have always loved) is, "I obviously need a time out. I'll be back in a couple minutes."

3) Now that you are alone, tell yourself you are so brave and then really experience what you are experiencing. Yes, this is scary. But you can do it. Really dive down in there and name what you are experiencing.

4) Now ask a question: Ask yourself, "What of this is mine and what is not?" "What is mine to control in th s situation and what is not?"

5) Now ask the next question: "What need do I have that is not being met?"

6) Figure out some way to meet that need if there is one. It may not be exactly what you want—it may be something you will get later. It may be a small thing when what you really want is big. But find something you can give yourself that meets your need in some small way.

7) On the other hand, if your breath goes into your belly when you do your initial check in, you are most likely experiencing a feeling. We usually brush these as de. They are usually a still, small voice and don't usually demand that we pay attention.

8) If it is a feeling, Practice The Pause Excuse yourself from the situation.

9) Once you're alone, ask this question: "What does this feeling need me to know?"

10) Figure out some way to acknowledge that feeling. It may be a small thing like just letting it know you hear it. Or it may be a big thing like changing your vacation plans or asking for more information before following throuch on a medical procedure. But do something to acknowledge the message you have received.

Owning our story and loving ourselves
through that process is the bravest thing
we will ever do
-Brene Brown

When we really experience our feelings and emotions
unapologetically, powerful things happen:

1) We strengthen our understanding of who we really are.

2) We disempower our overwhelming emotional responses,
leaving us less reactionary and more present.

3) We create a deeper bond of trust with ourselves and tune in
more and more to our deepest selves.

4) We create a stronger bond between ourselves and others
when they feel safer with us.

5) We encourage others that it is okay to experience their
emotions and feelings and truly express themselves.

6) We break the bonds of secret shame that locks us into
isolation and loneliness—which sets us free.

Each time you practice this, you get better at it. Soon it will be
your default and you will be able to do it quickly, even in the
most difficult situations. You are rewiring old, unhealthy patterns—
patterns of shutting down and not paying attention and then
exploding with a backlog or overwhelm of emotion. Or, just as
harmful, patterns of ignoring actual feelings that come from the
deepest part of what makes you truly you—feelings that are the
exact guideposts, and the exact amount of energy, that can lead
you to your most beautiful and fulfilling life.

CHAPTER 5

Loving Your Broken Places: How to Shift From Perfect and Disconnected, to Authentic and Deeply Connected

Worldwide, depression is the leading cause of disability, and
anxiety is the most common mental disorder according to
the Anxiety and Depression Association of America. And the
numbers are only increasing each year. There is not any one
reason that has been pinpointed as the root cause of these
two debilitating conditions, but there are many reasons that are
considered to be contributors: Genetics, high toxic load, lack
of essential nutrients, too much screen time, feeling lonely and
disconnected, spending less time in nature, etc.

One contributing factor that is often overlooked is perfectionism
and the isolation that typically goes along with that. I have seen
this tendency in myself and in my clients: If you are not open
about your messed up-ness, you will become more anxious and
disconnected, lonely and fearful as you desperately try to hide
the sad truth by putting a good face on it. A sad byproduct of
this is that others will have nothing to connect with—there will be
no way into the real you—nothing to grab onto. It's like trying to
grab a glass tube in a sink full of water—it may look pretty, but it
just slips right through your fingers. And, like a glass tube, when
we live this way, we are prone to shattering.

If you are simple and honest and open about your messed-up
places, you are more like a piece of pottery—so easy to hold
onto because there is texture and weight. And, like a piece of
pottery, we are less prone to breakage. Think about it: If you are
already all out there with everything you are, there is nothing to
hide. There are no secrets to spackle over with pretty Instagram
pictures. You can just be your whole self in any situation without
fear of someone figuring out some dirty little secret about you.

Every single client who has decided to live his or her life more this way—to fight against that perfectionism and just be out there with their whole, imperfectly perfect self—has found that many other people respond positively because they are so relieved to know that someone else deals with the same things they do. You are not alone! You only feel alone because no one is willing to take the first step out of that isolating box of perfectionism.

One of my favorite clients was a midwife. She had worked with hundreds of pregnant people and genuinely helped them through every kind of birth imaginable. She was great on social media and seemed to be very vulnerable and real when she posted. But she had a deep, dark secret: Both of her children had been born by Cesarean-section, so she had not herself gone all the way through a birth process without medical assistance. She lived in dread that others in her circle would find this out and expose her as a fraud. How could she guide others through their births when she had never "done it right" herself?

This secret made her afraid of any situation where she might be exposed. It made her feel like an imposter. She struggled to feel authentic and deeply connected with others, always fearing they might find out her deepest, darkest secret and shame her.

Finally, she decided living that way was worse than the fear of being judged and ostracized. She wrote a long blog post talking about her births and how she felt about them. Dozens of comments poured in from other people who shared their own stories of births that had not gone the way they wanted, of feeling judged, of always carrying around the feeling of being "less than." It was big and cathartic and life changing. My client's perception of her births shifted and her faith in the power of honesty grew. She became a role model for so many other people and impacted lives not just as a midwife, but as a beacon of living a fully realized life of vulnerability and authenticity.

Of course, there were the mean comments as well. There will always be those people who throw rocks and sling arrows. But that's the whole point: Those people are few, and they will always be there. Always. No matter what you do. Sooooo... it doesn't really matter if you try to appear perfect. Those people will still be there.

> You can never make everyone happy, so you might as well do what is best for you. Then at least one person will be happy.

CHAPTER 6

Clean Out Your Underwear Drawer: You Deserve Only the Best Underwear

I get the whole decluttering thing. I really do. Even more
than that, I get the power of creating a vacuum and being
dis-comfortable with the emptiness until you decide what, if
anything, you want to fill it up with.

But a new layer has emerged for me around this idea
decluttering and creating space. It began with Marie Kondo's
book, The *Life-Changing Magic of Tidying Up*. In her book,
she talks about holding each item you own and having a
conversation with it—really feeling its energy and asking it if it
still has a place in your life. If it has a purpose or is beautiful to
you or enhances your life in some way, then it stays. If it does
not, then it is released to find a new home.

I have used Kondo's technique in the past and it has helped me
feel good about passing items along for others to use that I had
been hanging onto for sentimental reasons or because I just
didn't know what I should do with them or I was afraid I might
need them "someday."

I was trying to use Kondo's life-changing magic on my
underwear one day. Now, things get pretty weird, pretty quick
when you start having conversations with your underwear. So,
instead, I was just taking each pair out of the drawer and culling
out the ones that had stretched out elastic or didn't look so
cute or didn't fit right. I found myself getting all tangled up in
this complicated inner dialogue that went something like this:
"Almost all of these are no good. But if I get rid of all of these, I'll
have like no underwear. Then what am I supposed to do? But
come on, April. You said you were going to do this. Just put all
of those in the To Go pile. Okay. That's good. How about these?
Well, these were really expensive I should keep them. But I've

never liked the way they fit. But they're really pretty. I never wear them. But they're really pretty and they were really expensive. Gah! Just put them on the bottom of the Keep pile and move on."

So many heavy emotions weighing down what should have been a simple process of cleaning out my underwear drawer! Layers of worry that I wouldn't have enough, anger that I had wasted money on things I didn't use, shame that I had let my things get in such disarray in the first place, an undercurrent of guilt that I had so much when so many have so little. Geesh.

How to get out of this quicksand of emotionally-based thoughts? Instead of fighting with them ('cause you will never win), I decided to just sit myself down on the bed in the middle of the piles of underwear and really feel all those feelings. Really feel them. And it sucked. It was complicated and embarrassing and felt like I was going to go down and never come back up. But as I sat feeling all of it, it began to loosen up so I could see it more clearly. Rather than a big wall of emotion, it spaced out enough that I could see each brick more clearly.

A lot of it was old and seemed like it was not even my stuff. It felt like I had been carrying around learned thoughts and behaviors from others. As I sat in those feelings, picking at that wall, I actually began to feel who some of those bricks belonged to. So I sat there and gave those bricks back to the people they belonged to. It wasn't easy because I had been carrying some of them around for years. It *felt right* that I would be carrying them. But, in my head, I just kept picking those bricks loose and gently handing them back to the person they belonged to. Some bricks belonged to my mom or my dad, my grandma or a friend. Some belonged to the church ladies of my childhood. Some to my first-grade teacher. Many of those people are not even alive anymore. But in my head, I just kept feeling myself picking up a brick, brushing it off, and giving it back to them anyway. With so much love.

I told them I loved them and I knew that they were strong enough to carry their own bricks now. That I am busy taking care of my own bricks so no one will ever feel the need to carry them for me, and I knew they could do the same.

And I felt the wall begin to crumble. Air began to move in and around the debris.

Now I could pick out even more individual bricks. Some of them were coping mechanisms from when I was younger and had fewer tools at my disposal. They were just misunderstandings about how things work or were cobbled together ways of dealing with difficult situations. Those were a little trickier to let go of because there was no one person to give them back to. And they were heavier because there was so much shame and guilt about how bad I had been at managing those situations. I should have been _____ (fill in the blank: Stronger, braver, smarter, more lovable, etc.). But I kept saying this Maya Angelou quote over and over in my head: "Do the best you can until you know better. Then when you know better, do better."

I found this hugely comforting. I began to feel some forgiveness for my younger self for not being perfect.

I lay down on the bed amidst my piles of underwear, saying to myself, "Grace and Space. Grace and Space." And, as I let myself breathe deeply and sank down into this strange, dis-comfortable space, I did find a little grace. That's all it took. Just a little Grace and a little Space, and that wall finally crumbled all the way down.

I felt a huge wave of energy course through me from my feet to the top of my head. I felt warm and safe and... dare I say it... happy.

I got up, wiped my eyes, and decided to just love myself. I

couldn't figure out what else would help and, hey, I had just done some really hard work. Loving myself looked like this: I decided I loved myself so much that I only wanted to give myself the most beautiful, most comfortable, most perfect underwear. I wanted to make sure that when I opened my underwear drawer, I could reach in with my eyes closed and pull out anything and be thrilled to put it on my body. That felt really radical. That felt scary and decadent and a little selfish.

But I tried it. Instead of culling out only the old and worn out, I went back through all the piles again and pulled out only the pieces I absolutely loved. I carefully folded the keepers and laid them neatly in my underwear drawer. I didn't let myself think. I just swept everything else into a bag and marched it out of my house and stuck it in the back of my car. "I'll deal with you later," I told the bag.

When I got back to my underwear drawer and pulled it open, I got choked up again—but this time with different emotions. There were five pairs of underwear and two bras. And I loved each and every one of them. I didn't feel guilty. I didn't feel scared. I didn't feel worried or selfish. I felt loved—loved that someone wanted me to have only the very best underwear.

A huge wave of happiness washed over me as I gently closed the drawer. Not only did I feel happy—I felt free. And clear. There was no blockage of energy around this anymore. I was clear on what exactly I liked and what I didn't. I would no longer make the same old mistakes by buying underwear that I did not love.

Another bonus from doing this: Months later, each and every time I open my underwear drawer—when I reach in without looking and put on something that I'm absolutely thrilled to put on my body—I still feel loved. I still feel treasured.

> Do the best you can until you know better.
> Then when you know better, do better.
> – Maya Angelou

So there ya go. Who knew there was so much to be learned from an underwear drawer.

DO THIS:

1) Clean out your underwear drawer.

2) Keep only those pieces you truly love.

3) Enjoy the ongoing happiness and love you feel from your awesome underwear drawer.

Notes:

CHAPTER 7

Nature Hates a Vacuum: How to Use This Truth to Your Advantage

There is a saying attributed to Aristotle that "Nature abhors a vacuum." This is true in my experience. What is also true is that this can be a very uncomfortable place to be: Airless emptiness. But here is the secret powerful people have learned: The ability to sit in that uncomfortable, airless vacuum is exactly what will create a vortex that will pull in new and amazing things you barely had the courage to dream of.

Think about it like this: You have a junk drawer. It is chock full of all sorts of stuff, everything from tools and rolls of tape, to tape measures and old phone cases. It is so full that you have to really work hard to squish even one more little thing in there. So you have this longing for something—something that would be so great to have in that drawer. Maybe you're really clear on what that something is, or maybe it's just a longing for... something. You keep thinking about this, daydreaming, maybe even researching or working toward it. But it just doesn't happen. No matter what you do.

The real problem here is that there is simply no room in that drawer. It seems really simplistic, but it is completely true: If you want to put something new in your drawer, you have to make a place for it to go.

Now imagine you want to create a big shift in your life. This is not just putting something small in a drawer—this is something major that needs to move. You can totally use Aristotle's axiom to your advantage. Instead of scheming and working and pushing to make this happen, you can:

1) Create a space. Either a physical space like emptying out a drawer or a cupboard, or a metaphysical space like ending an unhealthy relationship or quitting an energy-sucking job.

2) Sit in the discomfort of the emptiness. Sounds simple, but it can be very difficult to be jobless or unsure where you are moving or alone or...

3) Feel the power of emptiness as it begins to create a vortex. Feel the power of imagining all the possibilities that could fill up that empty space.

4) Wait until you are clear on what you REALLY want to fill that space up with.

When you first do this exercise, I suggest you practice this important and difficult skill on the physical level first. This will make it much easier to practice on the metaphysical level later on. It's simple: Empty a shelf or a drawer. Completely. Put everything that was there in the place it belongs or sell it/give it/donate it/throw it. Now, the more difficult part: Let it sit empty. This can feel really uncomfortable. That's okay. Notice what is most uncomfortable and just feel it. You will survive, I promise.

Or maybe you have the opposite experience: Maybe every time you look at your empty shelf or drawer, you feel a huge sense of relief like, "Oh wow. There's a little space right there! Aaaaaaahhhh."

Whatever you feel, just feel it.

Now begin to let your mind wander and play with the idea of what would like to be in that space. Maybe it wants to be a tea drawer with all sorts of delicious teas in little bags and containers, with lovely tea balls and pretty stirrers. Or maybe it's a showcase for all your beautiful handbags that have been tossed into various places all willy-nilly. Whatever you decide wants to live in this space you created, make it meaningful and purposeful—make it beautiful.

This is the same practice you can co with space you create in your mind, in your heart, in your hips, in your belly... in your LIFE.

Imagine how it would feel to open your closet or your cupboards—to look inside your mind or your heart—and find everything has been cleared out, freshened up, and made into a space you really want to inhabit.

An empty space creates a vortex that can pull in amazing new things!

Notes:

CHAPTER 8

⟨ ⟩

You May Be Missing the Full Power of This Gratitude Thing: Just One Little Change and The Power Will Be Unleashed!

Gratitude is definitely one of the most powerful tools in your arsenal. It is so powerful that just spending a minute or two a day thinking about what you are grateful can change your mood, your whole outlook on life, even your blood pressure.

Drs. Robert Emmons and Mike McCullough conducted a study in 2003 on gratitude. They had participants do one of three tasks: write down five things they were grateful that had occurred that week; write down five things they were having trouble with that week; or write down five events that occurred without guidelines about the events being positive or negative. Ten weeks later, participants in the gratitude group felt better about their lives as a whole and were 25 percent happier than the troubled group. They reported fewer health complaints and exercised an average of 1.5 hours more

That's pretty powerful. You can definitely improve your life by simply regularly writing down things you are grateful for. And if you go even further and use gratitude throughout your day as a practice—catching yourself in difficult situations or negative thought patterns and instead focusing on the things you are grateful for in those moments—the power grows exponentially.

But I want to share with you a simple way to totally amp your gratitude and increase your return on investment by ten-thousand-fold.

1) Make an agreement with yourself that you will spend just two minutes each day with your new gratitude practice. (You can do it! That's just two minutes of meditation and two minutes of gratitude once per day.)

2) On a blank piece of paper or clean page in your journal, write down one person or thing you are grateful for. That's it. Just one.

3) Now, list every reason you are grateful for that person or thing.

4) Make sure you list every reason.

5) Do the same thing on a fresh page tomorrow.

You may find that you can only think of a few reasons at first. You may have just two or three things listed and feel stuck. But dig a little deeper. Wait with your pen at the ready and take a deep breath down into your body and really think about why you are so grateful for this person or thing. Usually, you will find that your pen starts moving and doesn't want to stop. Often the tears start flowing, your heart opens wide and you find yourself flooded with a warm rush of love and gratitude that is like a much-needed rain on a dry field.

Soak it in. Let that rain pour down into every crevice and nourish your soul.

Making lists of people and things you are grateful for is a powerful practice. It connects you with your heart and does shift your thinking from the negative to the positive to some degree.

But rather than just making lists of people and things you are grateful for, take the time to dig down deeper and really feel your gratitude. Let it well up and pour out onto the page. It is in **the feeling** what you are grateful for that the real power lies. Doing your gratitude practice this way will shift your entire approach to life. You will be regularly overwhelmed by how darn lucky you are. You will not be able to believe, for instance, that you not only have this amazing body of your own to live in, but you have this whole other person to share this cup of coffee with. In fact, now that you notice it, you could write a whole page of reasons why you are grateful for that cup of coffee.

Once your heart bursts open into this deeper level of gratitude, even the most mundane things seem amazing!

Pro Tip: As you tap into this deeper level of gratitude practice, it can feel like you have attained a new way of life—like you're just a whole new person now. But it is actually a practice. If you do the normal human thing and, because you're feeling so good, start skipping a day here and there, you will find that it is all too easy to backslide into complacency. But, if you make this little practice an inviolable part of your day, you will reap exponential benefits. Two minutes. Every day. You'll be so grateful you did.

CHAPTER 9

The Secret of Affirmations

You can't tell yourself complete falsehoods and get away with it. You're smartest self—yes, the part of you that is actually completely in charge of helping you attain whatever it is that you desire—is way too smart to fall for some sort of canned affirmations like, "I love and approve of myself." Or "I am abundant. There is enough for everyone." Or (my personal favorite) "I am beautiful just the way I am."

Woop! Woop! WOOP! (That's your BS Meter going off.) All you have to do is look at your life or look in the mirror to know that none. of. that. is. true.

These canned affirmations (you can find hundreds of them just by doing a quick search for "best affirmations" or "top ten affirmations") will do little or nothing to help you. They will probably, sadly, cause you to feel like an even bigger loser because, good grief... you can't even do positive affirmations right.

I was around 30 years old when I first realized this affirmation thing would only work with the absolute truth. I was doing a practice of looking at my naked body in the mirror and trying to tell myself I loved myself and I was beautiful just the way I was. My BS Meter was going off the whole time. After years of body image issues compounded by an eating disorder and low self-esteem, this was a losing proposition. I tried saying the affirmations louder to drown out that other voice, but that other voice said, "Yeah, right. Anyone with eyes to see can tell that you don't *really* think you are beautiful just the way you are. You don't *really* love yourself. Not only do you not love yourself... You're also a big fat liar."

Yuck. Instead of replacing that voice with a more positive voice, I just ended up caught in the middle of a battle of warring voices that felt horrible and led me further down a negative rabbit hole.

I was trying to Stuart Smalley myself. (You know, that Saturday Night Live character who looks in the mirror and tells himself with dopey insincerity, 'I am good enough. I am smart enough. And, doggone it, people like me.").

But the only thing I could find to say to my body with absolute truth for the first few months I did this exercise was, "I love you for being able to take me for walks in nature."

Seems sorta lame, I know. But the important thing was that it was absolutely true. And what happened when I told my body this simple little truth over and over, was that my body loved hearing it. And because my body was so proud that it could do this little thing for me, I began wanting to walk more and more in nature. And my body got happier and healthier. And because it was happier and healthier, it became easier and easier to love it. This little love fest began to take on a life of its own. It grew stronger and stronger until I found one morning that I looked in the mirror and could say, with complete and total honesty, "Wow! Look at you, body. I love your long, strong, lean legs!"

Your body is starving for
kind, *truthful* words.

I could feel my body soaking in these new, deliciously loving and truthful words.

And the love fest between my body and myself has continued ever since. Sure, we have rocky moments—any love relationship does. But the foundation is strong because it is built on truth and trust and, therefore, survives these little moments with much more grace than it ever could have before.

DO THIS:

1) Spend a little time finding something you can affirm to yourself that is actually true.

2) Repeat it to yourself every single day as lovingly as you can.

3) As your relationship grows, add in more loving and truthful affirmations.

That's it. Simple. Profound.

CHAPTER 10

The Magic of Wanting a Cup of Coffee: The Subtle Art of Wanting What You Want

That cup of coffee you were so grateful for in Chapter 8? There is even more magic to be discovered in that ceramic cup of Joe.

My eight-year-old and I were driving to school one morning and she was pushing the automatic window button over and over. The window went up... the window went down... It was kind of driving me crazy, but she had a look on her face that was far away and curious so, instead of telling her to cut it out, I asked her, "What are you thinking over there?"

She said in a dreamy voice, "If I want the window to be open, I can just think to myself, 'I want the window open.' Then, all I have to do is push this button and it opens. I don't have to think, 'Okay, all you muscles, move my arm up just the perfect amount so my hand is right over the window button. Now, hand muscles, use just the right amount of force to push the window button just enough to open the window. And on and on like that. All I have to do is want the window open, and then everything just happens so the window is open. It's like magic!"

Huh. So true. It is like magic.

We forget this simple truth.

Everything is like that.

1) Want a cup of coffee. Or a cup of tea. Or whatever small thing you decide to want.

2) Go get yourself that thing that you want.

That's it. Done.

But now, take a few moments to notice that you did it. Notice that you just did a truly magical thing. You wanted something and BAM! You got it. That is so magical!

The secret is this: The more you notice how magical you are with smallish things like getting a cup of coffee or tea when you want it—the more you celebrate your magicalness with these smaller things—the more effective you will become at magically getting things you want that are not so smallish.

Try it and watch your magic grow.

Pro Tip: Humans are created to look for confirmation of our truths. We go through our days noticing every incident that affirms what we already think is true. We also, therefore, are very adept at not noticing, or dismissing, anything that contradicts our truths. So, use this human trait to your advantage. Be more purposeful in what you choose to notice! The more you step out of the rote noticing you normally do—the more you really notice the magicalness of ordinary things in your every day, the more magicalness there will be. This is a universal truth that any quantum physicist will tell you: You notice more of what you notice. To say it another way: If you want more magical things in your life, notice the magical things that are already in your life.

CHAPTER 11

Reality is What You Make Of It: Pay Attention to What You Want More Of

Let's dive deeper into this idea of noticing more of what we want more of.

I work with newborns every day. I watch how these precious, porous little beings are furiously gathering data through their bodies—through their senses. But the adults in their lives are just as furiously shaping (both consciously and unconsciously) what these little beings are thinking and feeling about this data. In fact, adults are shaping what data babies will even notice!

According to many scientists including Dr. Joseph Dispenza, "The brain processes 400 billion bits of information a second. But, we are only aware of 2,000 of those." In other words, "The human body sends 11 million bits of data per second to the brain for processing, yet the conscious mind seems to be able to process only 50 bits per second" (http://www.basicknowledge101.com/subjects/brain.html)

We are quite literally taught which of those 400 billion bits of information per second are worthy of our attention. Imagine a baby who is staring off into space. The adult either doesn't interact (because at least the baby isn't crying!), or they say things to the baby like, "Oh. You like those lights and shadows, don't you? Those shadows are so pretty, aren't they?" Well, maybe the baby was looking at something besides lights and shadows. Maybe the baby was looking at something the adult wasn't even conscious of. But the baby is now being conditioned that paying attention to lights and shadows gets you positive feedback, and noticing whatever else they might have been noticing, does not. Which do you think they are going to pay attention to going forward?

Think about that for a moment. Open your mind up to the possibility that what you are experiencing this very second as "reality" is actually severely limited. That in actuality, you are only experiencing a sliver of what is truly occurring all around you.

Danish physicist, Torr Norretranders converted how much data a human can process in bandwidth terms and completely confirmed this vast gulf between available data and our limited processing capabilities. David McCandless, in his famous TED Talk, visualized Norretranders' data and it looked similar to this:

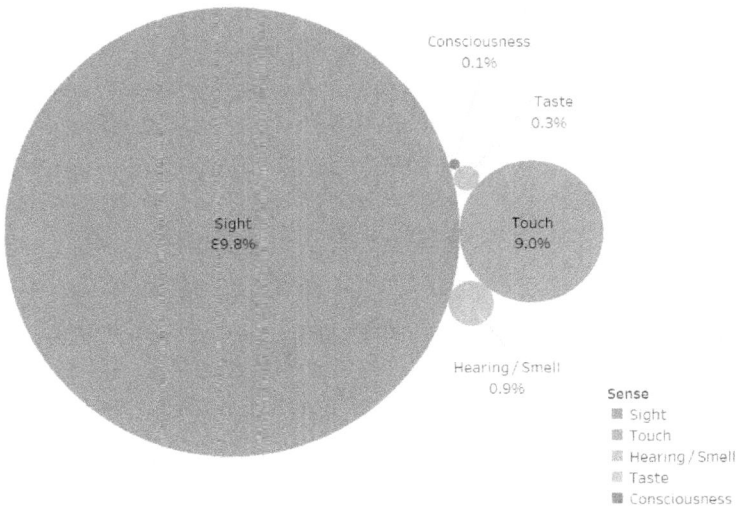

The big secret here is that you can, at least to a degree, override your conditioning and experience a bigger slice of reality or even a completely different reality. You can, in fact, have an active role in selecting what you experience as "reality."

There are some quick and simple ways to shift what you experience as your reality.

DO THIS:

1) Practice thinking that what you perceive as "reality" is really your interpretation of a very thin slice of "reality." Notice how you talk about both physical objects and experiences as if they are absolutes. Try getting curious and shifting that language to be more fluid and open-ended. There are a lot of books and articles available about this concept. Reading some of that material can help you open up your mind to new ways of thinking about reality too. But just purposefully shifting your thinking from "reality is a concrete/absolute thing" to "reality is way bigger than I can perceive and is, therefore, by its very nature, open to interpretation" can really change things.

2) Meditate every day (Chapter 1). This practice teaches your brain to remain calm and less emotional, even when in difficult or overwhelming situations that seem absolute.

3) Become aware of what you think about regularly. These repetitive thoughts work just like prayers (Chapter 24). They are sending out clear messages that you think those things are very important. If those thoughts are framed in the negative, as worries, then you are actually praying for those negative things to come to fruition. Notice when those thoughts start in your mind and practice shifting them from the negative (e.g., worries) into positives (e.g., prayers).

4) Take better care of your body so you receive broader and more accurate information. This includes giving your body fuel from nutritionally dense foods, getting enough sleep, feeding yourself uplifting and interesting information, and moving your body to help it clear toxins and stale energy.

Here's an example of how powerful point number four is: I recently had to take a round of heavy-duty antibiotics. I had not taken antibiotics for years, but there was no getting around it—I needed them this time. Two days after I finished the course of antibiotics, I hit a low point like I had not experienced in twenty years. I'm normally very adept at practicing good mental health: When negative, repetitive thoughts come up or I start worrying about something, I quickly replace those patterns with a healthier pattern. But this day, I felt as though the entire world was going up in flames. There was no redemption. Everything was pointless and downward and hopeless and ruined and... No matter how I tried, I could not shake this feeling.

And I really tried. I pulled out all my tricks: I sat quietly and tried to pinpoint where these feelings were coming from in my body. No go. I went for a walk in nature. Didn't budge the thoughts swirling in my head and the emotions churning in my gut. I fed myself nourishing and delicious food. It made me feel like throwing up. I talked it through with a friend, snot crying and wailing...but everything still felt horribly, horribly wrong.

Finally, I just went to bed and cried myself to sleep.

When I awoke the next morning, I made myself sit for my normal two minutes of meditation and prayer. And the answer smacked me upside the head: Those antibiotics had killed off all the healthy gut flora I had worked so hard to grow. My microbiome that was usually so healthy and friendly, was decimated and had not had time to grow back. Therefore, the messages I was getting from my body were all doom and gloom—lack and emptiness. As soon as I put this together, everything changed because I understood that the messages I was receiving were not "truth." They were only the temporary rantings of an overgrowth of bad bacteria. I knew I could take action to help my body get back in balance and that this would allow it to send me healthier messages. Two days of eating lots of fermented foods and taking some powerful probiotics had me right back in a better frame of mind.

So, I took action and helped myself experience a different reality by making my body healthier, which meant I received more positive messages from my body. You can do the same thing by helping your body be healthier. Remember the lesson of the Alula: Even the smallest change can yield big results. Maybe you cut out sodas, or take a walk at lunch instead of eating out of the vending machine, or eat a vegetable with every meal, or play pickleball with some friends once a week. Small changes can yield big results in the form of the messages you receive from your body.

We underestimate how interdependent our physical health and our mental/emotional health are. You can use this to your advantage: If you are suffering physically, try shifting your mental state by meditating or praying, reading, or watching something uplifting, talking to a friend, getting out into nature, etc. If you are suffering mentally/emotionally, try shifting your physical state by moving your body, getting out into nature, eating something deeply satisfying and/or nourishing, changing an unhealthy habit, eating fermented foods and/or taking a probiotic to feed the good bacteria in your gut, etc. It is amazing how much shifting one can impact the other.

You can take action to change your experience of reality in other simple ways too. Here is a little trick to train yourself to really believe that your reality is not static—that you see what you expect to see. This is one of my favorite exercises ever. I learned it from someone (I wish I could remember who so I could give them credit) over twenty years ago, and I still do it when I need to remind myself of how much of my "reality" is simply made up of what I choose to notice. It's super simple and totally mind blowing.

DO THIS:

1) How many yellow cars do you think you saw as you went about your day today? Two? Three? Maybe four?

2) Tomorrow, make a point of looking for yellow cars everywhere you go. Keep track of how many you see.

3) At the end of the day, tally up your total.

4) Crazy, right??

I have never asked anyone to do this exercise who didn't tell me, with complete and utter shock, that they couldn't believe how many yellow cars they saw when they made a point of looking. They always ask me, "Was I somehow calling in yellow cars because I wanted them to be there?" Then they say, "Or maybe all those yellow cars were there all along and I just didn't notice them because I wasn't looking for them?"

I believe it is some beautiful combination of those two ideas—prayers (things we purposefully ask for like seeing lots of yellow cars) get answered, for sure (Chapter 24). So maybe there were actually more yellow cars to be seen because you asked to see them. Or maybe they were there all along, and you just weren't paying attention to them. But the bottom line is the same whichever of these is true.

What else do you think could be around you all day long that you don't even notice?

You can play with this exercise using anything you want. Get curious. Try out different things and see what happens. This little exercise can open up whole new versions of reality!

What if you decided to see how many ways the world showed you love today?

You would notice when the traffic lights turned green just as you approached them so you could roll into work right on time. You would notice the person with the full shopping cart who kindly moved to the next lane over so you could scoot into the empty lane with your three items. You would notice the soft breeze as it tickled your cheek on the walk back to your car. You would notice that the airline ticket you've been watching just unexpectedly dipped below your low-price alert.

You would feel so loved.

Notes:

CHAPTER 12

Let's Play the "What If" Game

There are times when a client gets on my table and their body is literally vibrating. It feels like my hands are on a dam that is barely able to hold back a massive, up-swelling wave. I love these moments, even though my client may not be enjoying it so much. For the client, it feels like he or she is stuck—like no matter what they do, nothing seems to flow. They work so hard at everything, thinking that hard work will make things work better. But the truth is that hard work is not the missing element. The missing element is getting up and out of the space of "I must control everything in order to make it work."

When we get caught in this space, we can only work with our own limited resources. And we are completely blocked by our own fears and feelings of limitation. It's like you know you have a Rembrandt dying to come out of you, but you think you are only allowed to work with those five big, fat kindergarten crayons. You keep trying. You try harder. And harder. You are now a master of every single thing those fat crayons are capable of. But you are left feeling completely frustrated because they simply cannot bring into reality what your soul is longing to create.

And that's the secret. You cannot create your soul's desires with your own limited resources. You need to step into the space of creative play with the master Creator.

And the easiest way to access this magical space is to play a simple little game of "What if...??"

1) Think of something in your life that you long for that doesn't feel delicious and flowing. This may be something you have been working on for a long time, or it might be a new thing that you've just started to desire.

2) Imagine this something as an actual object that is sitting right in front of you. For instance, if you have been longing to travel to an exotic destination, imagine a lovely box with a beautiful souvenir from your trip inside.

3) Now think of all the reasons why you cannot pick up that lovely box. Maybe you're worried about how to pay for it, or have concerns about specifics like missing work, what people will think of you, your expired passport, etc.

4) And now the fun part: In your mind, just pick up the box. That's it. Just reach forward and pick it right up. Put it in your lap and open it. Imagine pulling out the beautiful souvenir from your trip. Don't let your mind tell you all the reasons you cannot have this beautiful gift. Just pull it out and feel it in your hands. Feel how happy your heart is at having this thing you have been longing for. Feel how grateful you are that you have been given this beautiful gift.

5) Now, play the "What if..." game. What if this could really happen? What if you could have this thing you have been longing for? What if the worst thing you can think of happening didn't happen? What if the very best thing you can think of happening happened?

There is absolutely no reason the worst-case scenario you can imagine is any more of a reality than the very best-case scenario. Absolutely no reason at all.

The only thing standing between you and the best-case scenario is your own limited beliefs. Those beliefs are what keeps you trying to create your masterpiece with those five fat Crayons. Those beliefs are the dam between you and the massive, up-swelling wave of everything your soul desires.

Any time you find yourself feeling stuck or limited or frustrated with a current situation, just play the "What if...?" game. Those two little words invite the infinite wisdom of the Universe to co-create with you the exact reality you are long for.

WHAT IF...
everything was going to be okay?
Or even great?

Notes:

CHAPTER 13

Three Powerful Little Words: Key to Navigating the Most Difficult Situations

It had been a tough couple of months. My husband and I were passing each other in the hallways because we were working ridiculous hours, our family schedule was hectic and scheduled to the minute, finances were a problem, our eleven-year-old had started having episodes no one could explain where she would just stop breathing and have to be rushed to the hospital, our nephew was having a rough time and living with us, and I was still working with five to seven people a day... I was holding on by a thread and my body was breaking down. I had gotten away from most of my good habits: I was not exercising, I was grabbing food and eating it in the car, I was going a hundred miles an hour every day until I collapsed into bed. I felt disconnected and downright horrible.

The one good habit I clung to was my two minutes of meditation every day. As I sat myself down one morning for that two-minute meditation, something snapped. Something inside me rose up and screamed for help. I lay down on the floor and wept, "Please help me. I'm so scared and overwhelmed and nothing is working right no matter how hard I try. Please. Please, help me." I lay there, prostrate on the floor, waiting for a wave of comfort or words of wisdom. And a small voice whispered in my ear, "It doesn't matter."

Oh, I was angry. I sat up and dried my tears. I stood up and stomped through my day, muttering the whole time, "I asked for help. Seriously? That's what I get? 'It doesn't matter?' What the hell is that even supposed to mean??"

When I finally collapsed into bed that night, I was still seething. Of course all of the things I was doing and managing and scheduling and failing at all mattered a lot. But as I lay there, desperately trying to fall asleep, I noticed something. It was a tiny bit easier to breathe. Huh. Interesting. I took a little bit deeper breath and noticed my chest felt a bit more relaxed. What was this? It was a relief and I wanted more. As I took in an even deeper breath, that small voice whispered in my ear again, "It doesn't matter."

Oh, the tears as the true meaning of this finally soaked in! Weight fell off my chest as I heaved and sobbed. I felt like a glacier was cracking and huge chunks of ice were falling away. I lay in the bed and just wailed out all of the pain and fear and loneliness and "Nothing I do ever works out" and "What am I doing wrong." My breath got deeper, my body got softer, and a gentle, restful sleep enveloped me.

When I woke the next morning, my mind did not immediately jump onto the hamster wheel and start spinning out all of the million moving parts I had to manage that day, the credit card debt I didn't want to face, the truth that I was a total imposter which I better keep hidden. Instead, I found myself snuggling back down into the warm covers and whispering to myself over and over, "It doesn't matter."

Sweet relief. I moved through that day with the whisper in my ear at every turn. Didn't have milk for the cereal the kids wanted: "It doesn't matter." Make them eggs and toast instead. Double-booked two clients: "It doesn't matter." Apologize sincerely and get hugs from both for being human and making mistakes. Hit a pole while backing up in the grocery parking lot: "It doesn't matter." Chalk it up to moving too quickly and go a little slower and more consciously for the rest of the day.

This powerful little phrase has become my constant mantra. At first, I used it with small things like milk and scheduling snafus. But, quickly, I found myself whispering it under my breath with big things too.

Our daughter was not feeling well one night and got herself into a bath. I was on high alert as we still had no answers for why she was having the episodes where she couldn't breathe. Sure enough, I checked on her and her face was a deep blue. Her head lolled back on the edge of the bathtub and her eyes rolled back in her head. "Can you breathe?" I yelled. She shook her head "No" with bulging, terrified eyes.

Her whole body was now blue, her eyes were bright red, and I started trying to get her slippery 90-pound body out of the tub. Somehow, we dragged/carried her down the hall and threw her in the car. Our older daughter called the hospital to alert them we were coming in, and I drove 100 miles per hour to get her there. Every time I looked over at her, she was barely conscious. I slapped her and said, "Stay with me! Stay here. Come back!" and she whispered, "I love you, Mama."

As they threw her in a wheelchair and took her pulse ox. As they told me her oxygen level was a 64. As they rushed her into a room and worked to revive her. Through the entire thing, there it was: The small, insistent voice whispering in my ear—"It doesn't matter."

And it's the truth. In the strangest way, it doesn't matter. My daughter could have died. I could have been completely unable to save her. And all of it would have been devastating. Nearly impossible to recover from. But, ultimately, life would have gone on. In the long run, things would have healed as best they could, and I would have been a new version of okay.

It may sound callous to you at first—it did to me. "What do you mean, "It doesn't matter?? It totally matters. I totally care about this!"

But the hard truth is this: We are never in control of most things. Never. We love to tell ourselves we are. We comfort ourselves by controlling small things like how much food we eat or how much money we spend. We set up elaborate structures with our houses and cars and other belongings, our schedules and friend lists to make it look like we are in control. But the truth is that most things are never truly in our control.

This is a super scary thought. Brushing up against this reality makes most of us so uncomfortable, we run screaming back into our seemingly safe little shells where we can pretend we are in control.

But as I settled into the idea of "It doesn't matter"—as it became a constant in my mind—in a strange way, it began to free me. It was releasing me from the need to be in control of every little thing. I felt weight falling off my shoulders with each repetition of the phrase.

And the most beautiful outcome of internalizing this little phrase is that I have found I can actually go deeper. When I practice the truth of "It doesn't matter," I can show up fully in situations where, in the past, I would have had to protect myself, kept a part of myself separate, or have not even been able to be in some situations because they were just too difficult to manage.

Thanksgiving of 2016, my father let us know that something was horribly not right with his body. He wasn't sure what was going on yet, but it was not going to be a best-case scenario. Having lost my mother to ovarian cancer when I was four years old, this was tough to hear.

As we stepped into the fast/slow walk through a year and a half of diagnosis, treatment, and the slide into death, I clung to my mantra. "It doesn't matter," I whispered to myself as I watched my father's athletic, 6' 3' body wasting away. "It doesn't matter," I sobbed as I rubbed his freezing cold, bony feet for the five-hundredth time. "It doesn't matter," I breathed out through chattering teeth in those final, horrible hours when his spirit was finally released from its shell.

> Get very clear about what is in your control.
> Control it.
> Find a way to let the rest go.

I certainly did not have control over the fact that my dad got cancer. Or that he died a slow and painful death. But I did have control of my own emotions. With the help of "It doesn't matter," I was able to let go of what was not mine and take good care of what was. This allowed me to be 100 percent present for my father's last months on earth. I was able to show up all day, every day, for so many days, and really be there with him. I was able to have hard conversations and hear him process really difficult truths. And I would have missed all of that—or have only been partially present because of needing to protect myself—if I had not been steeped in "It doesn't matter."

When I totally embrace "It doesn't matter," I am able to let go of needing to control things that are not—never were—mine to control. This, in turn, allows me to more clearly see those few things that are in my control and have the energy to take care of them appropriately.

And when I actually take care of the things that are mine to control, as difficult as that can be, it makes it easier to let go of the things that are not mine to control, which gives me more energy to take care of the things that are mine to control, which allows me to...well, you get the idea.

CHAPTER 14

Whomever or Whatever is Most Unlovable, Needs the Most Love

Whomever or Whatever is Most Unlovable, Needs the Most Love

About two months after I gave birth to my first baby, I called my grandma because I was totally losing it. Overwhelmed and exhausted, I hadn't showered in days, and I felt like my only purpose in life was to be a slave to that little creature's every need...and she could be so demanding. And so cranky!

I expected words of sympathy. A little commiseration. After all, my grandmother had raised five babies of her own, so surely she knew what I was going through. But what I got instead was this: "When that baby girl is the crankiest—when she is the most unlovable—that is exactly when she needs your love the most."

Ugh. That wasn't what I was looking for at all. But it was exactly what I needed to hear. I needed help reframing my situation from "I must be doing something wrong because this baby is not happy," to "I am doing everything exactly right because this baby is not happy." Once I got out of the feeling of guilt, the feeling of "I'm not enough," and "I'm not the right mother for this baby, obviously," I began to think of it like this: Baby Girl is challenging. Thank goodness I am patient and loving and have the ability to be completely available to her. She has the exact right mother for her cranky little self.

The side effects of this shift were monumental. I felt calmer and happier with myself because I was now succeeding at parenting a challenging baby. I was no longer gauging my own failure or success on her contentedness. This meant I could congratulate myself for just consistently showing up and loving her the best I could even though it was really difficult. I began allowing her to be with other people more because I wasn't afraid she would be happier with other people than with me—if that kid could be happy for a little while with anyone, I was going to just be happy about it!

It also meant that I was doing the important work of acknowledging that, while we were deeply bonded, there was differentiation between myself and my baby. This is not a popular concept in our society. We are taught that proper bonding entails being one with our babies. That it is best to subsume ourselves into our parenting and let those lines between ourselves and our little ones get so blurry that they practically disappear. This leaves us, as parents, in the unfortunate position of feeling like we don't exist as ourselves anymore. I hear from new parents every day that they feel like they are horrible people if they are away from their babies for a minute, that they don't sleep, forget to eat, are wracked with guilt and overwhelm and don't even feel like they are parenting well. And, thanks to social media, also feeling like, somehow, everyone else is doing it all so beautifully—even effortlessly.

The cure for these feelings of guilt and inadequacy is to be clear that bonding is not the same as being subsumed. There is meant to be space in every relationship. (Let's be clear though: those first three months or so with a new baby is different. Those months are just surviving however you can because there really is NO space between you and your baby. There is not meant to be. Nature has set it up that you are still your baby's entire universe.) As our children get a little older, there is meant to be a natural progression that includes learning where you end and they begin It is important work for us as parents, and an essential skill for children to learn as well.

The other thing I was learning was to really love myself. As much as I was doing a better job of loving my baby when she was least loveable, I was also starting to do a better job of loving myself. Even when I felt overwhelmed and guilty and less-than—actually, especially at those times—I was doing better at just being loving to myself. Each time I found myself slipping back into the overwhelm and guilt, I would say:

> When I am least loveable is when
> I need the most love.

DO THIS:

1) Start to notice when you are talking meanly to yourself or feeling inadequate/less-than/ impatient/mean/overwhelmed/ worried/anxious/_____ (fill in the blank).

2) Just say these words to yourself: "When I am least loveable is when I need the most love."

3) If you have a child or children, teach them teach them to do this too.

CHAPTER 15

❧

Grow Some Boundaries

Most people think of boundaries as walls. But walls are restricting. And nobody wants to feel restricted. Think of all the inspirational quotes about breaking through walls, tearing down fences, and growing bigger than the field you've been constrained in. "Don't fence me in!" Nobody would be interested in boundaries if they are like fences.

Others think of boundaries the other way around: It's not that you are penned in, but that you are keeping things out. These people think having boundaries means saying "No" to things, that it means holding others at arm's length. Nobody would want to have boundaries that make for a smaller life—even if it means minimizing overwhelm and/or the possibility of getting hurt.

Neither of these are my experience with boundaries at all. In fact, boundaries have done the exact opposite for me.

I do not think of boundaries as restricting or limiting. I think of them more like the edges of a bouncy house—I can go crazy inside there without any concern of hurting myself because all that will happen is that I get gently bumped back into the middle when I try to bounce too far or too high.

The other important thing to note about having good, strong boundaries is that they are not static. You can redraw, reshape, make carve outs and even escape doors any time you want! But if they are good, strong boundaries, you will do this with consciousness. It will not just be willy-nilly with you bouncing all over the place and breaking your leg and landing on your head. It will be purposeful and make sense that you want to grow bigger in this one area—and that your boundaries need to be adjusted to allow you room to grow.

When you have strong fences, you are free to run with total abandon inside them.

1) Think of an area of your life where you feel taken advantage or not appreciated.

2) Really feel all the feelings around that: Anger, frustration, sorrow, jealousy, invalidation, etc.

3) Now think what would help you feel protected in this situation. What would be like the walls of a bouncy house so you could be free inside those smooshy walls?

4) Enact those things that would help you feel protected.

Please note: Sometimes the smartest action is to remove yourself from circumstances that could cause you harm. This is intelligent and correct. The goal you are working toward here is not to stay in dangerous situations when it is within your power to remove yourself. No The goal here is to be able to be okay in difficult or even dangerous situations over which you have no control.

CHAPTER 16

A New Way of Thinking About Attention Deficit Disorder: It May Not be What You Think

At this point in time, most everybody has a broad understanding of what Attention Deficit Disorder (ADD) is. It was acknowledged as a disorder by the American Psychiatric Association in 1968 and has been increasing in prevalence ever since. 12.9 percent of men will be diagnosed with an attentional disorder over their lifetime, and 4.9 percent of women will be diagnosed, according to the Attention Deficit Disorder Resource Center's reporting in 2014.

Symptoms include:

- Decreased cognitive function, particularly making careless mistakes and inattention to details

- Having problems sustaining attention on tasks

- Do not seem to be listening when being spoken to

- Difficulty following instructions

- Lack of motivation

- Organization is difficult

- Resistance to starting and finishing tasks that require mental energy

- Losing belongings frequently

There is a new school of thought suggesting that some percentage of what is diagnosed as ADD might actually be clinical exhaustion. So many of us are stressed, work long hours, don't eat well, don't exercise, and sleep too little or don't sleep deeply. ADD and clinical exhaustion share the same symptoms, which certainly begs a closer look.

Also of note is that traumatized people experience many of the same symptoms as ADD and clinical exhaustion. The National Institute of Mental Health estimates that 3.6 percent of Americans suffer from Post-Traumatic Stress Disorder (PTSD). The actual incidence is likely much higher as many people suffering in this way will not seek out professional help and, therefore, go undiagnosed.

But I would like to throw another hat in the ring. Open your mind for a moment and imagine with me what it would feel like to be an infant/child when: You are always shushed; you're made to sleep in an empty room alone; told you are too much; touched in anger; touched rarely with kindness; made to sit still at a desk and pay attention for seven or more hours a day, five days a week; sent home to do more hours of work; have your worth judged by whether you do this work to someone else's standards which you may or may not even understand; fed nutrient-poor food that often includes stimulants like sugar or caffeine; not taught techniques to help soothe and calm your mind and body; you try unsuccessfully to get your parents to look at you and play with you instead of paying attention to their work, their chores, or their devices.

Philosophers from Aristotle to Hegel, anthropologists and mental health professionals, medical doctors and poets have all emphasized that humans are, by nature, social animals. We actually have special neurons that allow us to match our emotions to another's. These "mirroring" neurons are believed to be the foundation upon which all social connection is built. It is an unconscious ability that is supposed to be activated when we are newborns interacting with the grownups in our lives. So, imagine the damage when these neurons are not activated early in life. Then feel the shunning and isolation that is layered on throughout childhood and on into adulthood.

If this was your life, I am pretty sure you would agree with me that you would be suffering from a lack of connection—a lack of loving attention. You would, in fact, be suffering from a deficit of attention—an Attention Deficit Disorder.

I would like to further suggest that in this way of thinking about Attention Deficit Disorder, the diagnosis is on a continuum rather than an either/or. You could have a mild case that would be easy enough to remedy, or a more severe case that would take serious work to turn around. There are no studies on this specific theory to date, but many studies have been done on the importance of being fully present for another person—on the power of giving someone your undivided attention.

There are also countless studies on the positive effects of human touch on everything from anxiety to depression, high blood pressure to hormone imbalance.

Just a few of the powerful positive impacts of human touch are:

1) Releases the oxytocin hormone. Called the "love hormone," oxytocin's job is to help you feel connected to others and promotes a sense of overall well-being and happiness.

2) Reduces production of cortisol, the "stress hormone."

3) Inspires optimism, positive thinking, and compassion.

4) Relieves anxiety and stress by increasing levels of dopamine and serotonin, two neurotransmitters that help regulate mood as well as good sleep patterns.

5) Lowers heart rate and blood pressure.

6) Increases immune system function.

7) Stimulates the hippocampus (the part of the brain that deals with memory).

Tiffany Field, a leading touch researcher, way back in 1998, called for "a shift in the social-political attitude toward touch." Humans have yet to embrace (pun intended) the idea that touch makes a positive impact and can be used as a powerful tool, not just for connection, but for simple resets of hormone levels, cognitive function, stress reduction, immune system boosting... the list goes on and on

To illustrate this point: One study found that when teachers touched young students on the shoulder, the children became more involved in their work and were 60 percent less disruptive in class (Wheldall, et al. 1986). The positive aspects of their behavior increased after being touched as well. They were 20 percent more likely to check their work for accuracy and 20 percent more likely to take a book home to read.

You can be ahead of this curve with yourself and your loved ones. You can purposefully use attention and touch to improve Attention Deficit Disorder and all the symptoms that can accompany it.

DO THIS:

1) Go through the symptoms of ADD listed above and rate yourself for each one on a scale of 1 (least) to 10 (most).

2) Keep a one-day personal connection diary. Write down each time you are present for someone or they are present for you. Note each time you are touched or touch someone else during this period—this includes everything from a handshake to a meaningful conversation and everything in between.

3) Now begin working to increase both the quality and the quantity of times you are connecting with and/or touching someone.

4) Now keep a three-day personal connection diary as you implement all of the ways you worked out to increase the amount of connection you experience.

5) Go back through the ADD symptoms and see how your numbers have changed.

Remember: Touch does not have to be somebody else touching you. It could be you touching someone else. It also does not have to be with a significant other, or even with another human being. Studies have shown that the same benefits occur whether you are sharing touch with a significant other, an acquaintance, a friend, a pet...or even yourself.

Let me say that last part again, because it is very important: You can achieve the same benefits by giving attention to yourself. Writing in your journal, reading something that inspires you, sitting down to a nice lunch with yourself, taking a walk in nature, body scrubs, facials, nail care, hair care, foot rubs, etc., are all things you can do for yourself that will positively impact your Attention Deficit Disorder and help you be a healthier, more connected and happier person.

There is not much in this world that cannot be improved upon simply by knowing someone cares about you—even if that someone is you.

CHAPTER 17

Deep Listening: Like Medicine for the Soul

Another way we show care is by being truly present.

When was the last time you felt truly listened to? Do you remember how it felt? Do you remember what the person did that made you feel so heard?

This is a dying skill that we desperately need to revive.

Sitting with women while they are giving birth has been my best teacher in the art of deep listening. You can't really have a normal conversation with someone in labor, so you have to get really good at listening in other ways. Noticing the subtle unspoken communications like a faintly furrowed brow or a turning away of the head when a certain person enters the room. Seeing their reactions when a word is spoken or a touch is given—watching them open up or shut down depending on the intent as well as the execution.

What I have learned from hundreds and hundreds of hours spent in this way, is that there are some specific things one can do that enhance listening—and really help a person feel heard.

Hallmarks of Deep Listening:

- Mirror the teller's body language and match their tone as closely as you can.

- Do not interrupt.

- Do not correct—even if something seems inaccurate or untrue. (Remember, it feels true to the teller.)

- Nod or make sounds or small comments only to encourage the speaker to continue.

- Be mindful of your body language—stay open and be careful of even small facial expressions that could be interpreted as judgment.

- Be mindful of the teller's body language—notice when the teller becomes tense or shut down. What was she saying at that moment?

- Let there be empty spaces in the telling—silence can feel awkward but is sometimes necessary to unearth deeply buried truths.

- When the teller is finished, tell them what you heard them say as much in their own words as you can, and then ask them if you got it right. An easy phrase to get you started with this is, "What I really hear you saying is _____. Is that right?"

- Always remember that this is not about you. Even if it is about you, remember that this telling is not about you. This moment is about the teller being allowed to have and share their experience and be fully heard.

- Do not judge.

- If you feel yourself being drawn in and/or triggered, remind yourself that this is not about you. If you are still finding it difficult to be a neutral listener, let the teller know that it is not because of them, but you need to excuse yourself. Try not to judge yourself. Just note that you have some work to do in this area and vow to do that work so you can be a better deep listener in the future.

Everyone wants to be seen –
and heard.

Being deeply listened to is a gift—a gift that can help a person feel less depressed, less confused and overwhelmed, less alone, more seen, more alive. If you can give this gift to someone else, you will provide a powerful healing opportunity for them. If you are given this gift yourself, enjoy the benefits and count yourself truly lucky.

Pro Tip: You can do this for yourself and it can be just as powerful. When was the last time you really listened to yourself? When was the last time you listened to yourself so thoroughly that you were practicing all of the hallmarks listed above? (That one about no judgment is particularly tough when we are listening to ourselves.)

Imagine how good it would feel—how healing it would be—if you just really listened to yourself instead of editing or correcting all the time.

Do This:

1) Make a quiet moment for yourself.

2) Tune in to something that you have been thinking about a lot.

3) Tell yourself that you really want to hear yourself out on this issue.

4) Go ahead and share about it.

5) Deeply listen to yourself, utilizing all of the good Hallmarks of Deep Listening listed above. All of them.

6) Notice how you feel once you are done with your telling and listening.

If you give yourself the gift of deeply listening to yourself on a regular basis, you will be calmer, your brain will be clearer, you will feel less overwhelm and anxiety, and you will be better able to offer the gift of deep listening to others.

Notes:

CHAPTER 18

Practice Good Mental Health

Did you know that studies show that a small pleasant event—just an everyday nicety—boosts your immune system for two days?

How strongly do every-day happy events affect you? One study indicates that a small pleasant event boosts the immune system for two days, while a small, everyday stressful event depresses the immune system for just one day.

Dr. Arthur Stone, a psychologist at Stonybrook University, conducted a research study with 100 men, measuring the effects of fun get-togethers with friends and family on the immune system. Dr. Stone found that the positive effect of a party on Friday lasts until Sunday. But, interestingly, a stressful event like being criticized at work on Monday, will only depress the immune system until Tuesday.

This study focused on the effects of ordinary, smaller life events on everyday life, not on long-term or sudden acute stressful or joyful events. The men recorded in a diary their everyday pleasures, such as socializing, or pursuing a hobby such as fishing. They also recorded stressful events, such as too heavy a workload, everyday hassles, being sick of chores and critical bosses. Their immune response was measured by daily samples of their saliva.

The happy social events and the pursuit of relaxing hobbies such as fishing engendered the best immune response boost, keeping a positive response for two full days, while the negative criticism depressed the immune response for only one day. When the men reported cold symptoms, there had been an increase in stressors three to five days before the symptoms of a cold came on, which is the incubation period for the cold virus.

But what was most interesting was that a drop in pleasurable events predicted a cold more readily than an increase in negative events.

You can totally use this human trait to your advantage. This tool is so simple and offers such a huge return on a minimal investment, you would have to be a fool not to purposefully harness its power.

Since it is clear that not just your mental health, but your physical health as well, is driven by small pleasant events with long-lasting results:

just make sure you do more and more small and pleasant things.

You will reap days of improved immune function and a stronger sense of well-being. You will also counteract any negative events that occur by stacking the odds in your favor.

The negative events are not always in your control so don't even try to control them. Just do more of what is absolutely in your control: create lots and lots of small, positive events and interactions throughout your day. Stockpile positive experiences!

Although there is not a study I can find to confirm this, I have seen it within myself and with my clients: The same is true of positive thoughts, not just positive events. The more positive thoughts you have, the happier and healthier you will be. And those positive thoughts are much more impactful and longer-lasting than the negative ones.

You can totally use this to your advantage as well. Your thoughts are not just random things that float through your consciousness. You actually have a say in what thoughts you think. You can catch yourself thinking something negative, and just replace

> Your thoughts are not the boss of you.

it with something positive. You can. Really. This is what I call Practicing Good Mental Health.

DO THIS:

1) Purposefully think more positive thoughts. When you have a few minutes in line or you're driving to work or whatever, rather than getting on your phone or worrying about bills or making a grocery list in your head, purposefully notice the beautiful sunrise, or think lovely thoughts about someone you love, or think about an event you enjoyed or that you're looking forward to.

2) Catch yourself thinking negative things. Try to catch yourself doing this as early as possible and purposefully replace those negative thoughts with positive ones.

It is really refreshing to live in a head that feels more up-beat and breezy. It is really powerful to realize that those negative repetitive thoughts don't just happen to you—you actually get to curate what goes on in your own head. This takes some consistent energy and feels foreign at first. But stick with it. It doesn't take long before you will notice, "Huh! I am thinking positive thoughts all the time now!" Remember: The profound and long-lasting results of Practicing Good Mental Health are really worth the effort.

CHAPTER 19

Give Yourself Some Grace
and Space

There is one concept I talk about with my clients a lot. I call it the Threshold Theory, and there are two ways to think about it.

The first is that nothing operates in isolation. So many things get the blame for the whole situation. But, in reality, they were just the straw that broke the camel's back. Food allergies often work this way.

So often people are diagnosed with a food allergy—let's say dairy, for example. On the one hand, it's a relief to have an answer to why they've been feeling so horrible for so long. But, on the other hand, their lives are now so much more complicated because avoiding dairy is not an easy thing to do. They certainly trigger on the tests as allergic to dairy, but I have seen an interesting phenomenon many times. It goes like this:

I say to my client, "How does it feel to have this allergy?" And they answer that it's frustrating and limiting. I say, "I have this curiosity about your allergy. I wonder how your body would be with dairy if it didn't have so many other toxic elements to deal with." And we begin to go through some of the sources of toxins in their life. We start with the common culprits like commercial meat and dairy, pesticide-laden fruits and vegetables, toxic household cleaning supplies, body products, hair care products... and they begin to get overwhelmed. "It seems like there's nothing that is okay!" they cry.

And then I introduce the second interpretation of The Threshold Theory. This idea is really simple but also profound:

Anything we do that is better, is that much better. Even if it is a little thing...we are still that little bit better.

And it buys us a bit of leeway for those things we can't (or don't) do better.

That is giving ourselves Grace and Space. And Grace and Space is like salve for our tired souls.

Part of the problem is that most of us are maxed out all the time. We are running our engines so fast and so hot, that our indicator lights are one hair away from the red zone at all times. The goal is to do everything in our power to bring that level down as low as we can get t—every chance we get—so that when we have no choice but to make a not-so-great choice, it will not put us right into that red.

Let's take water for example. I teach my students and my clients that water (like everything else in life) operates on a hierarchy: Any water is better than no water. Any filter is better than no filter. A filter that takes out heavy metals and bigger toxins is better than one that only takes out heavy metals. A filter that takes out all of that and hormones is better than one that does not. Etc.

So, when you have control over your source of water, make the best possible choice you can make within your means. Every time you do this, you buy yourself a little headroom for when you don't have control and need to make a lesser choice.

And let's give ourselves a little Grace when we cannot make the best choice. If your finances or relationships or time or whatever cause you to make a less optimal choice, forgive yourself, vow to make a good choice on something else that you have more control over, and then... Let. It. Go. Let yourself rest in the knowledge that you have a bit more headroom to spare from all those other more optimal choices you made.

DO THIS:

1. Make a list of the things you eat, breathe, put on your body, clean your home with, etc.

2. Check out the ingredients for as many of those things as you can. You can go to ewg.org to check the level of toxicity for most commercial products and all ingredients.

3. Get creative about how you can change some of the more toxic things for less toxic. Think about how much headroom you will buy with each of these changes. Pinterest is a great resource for inexpensive and easy replacements for most common products including laundry detergent, household cleaning supplies, etc.

4. Congratulate yourself for every tiny improvement you make because you are lowering your threshold and buying yourself more leeway for the things you do not have control over.

Do the very best you can every time you can.
This is like money in the bank for
when you can't.

CHAPTER 20

A Simple Meditation

We have explored the idea that our experience of reality is severely limited as well as highly selective, depending on our early influences and our ability to handle input. If you have read this book up to this point, it is not a new concept to you by now that your "reality" is nothing more than what you give the most attention to.

What you give the most attention to becomes your normal. It becomes comfortable. It feels correct. Even if it is not pleasant or what you really want, it still feels correct.

This is true on a psycho-emotional level for sure. People say things all the time that reinforce this concept: "Don't waste your time and energy dreaming about things that are never going to happen." "Get your head out of the clouds." "You have to live in reality."

Over time, this becomes true on a physical level as well. As you think the same thoughts, believe the same beliefs, you literally deepen the circuitry that runs between those synapses in your brain. Every single time you think the same thought, you deepen that trench. This is why it feels like "reality." This is why, even though you may be sick of your current situation, it feels correct. Because you so easily fall into that deep trench, it feels like truth.

But that trench is no more true—no more reality—than any other synaptic pathway. It's just easier to fall into because it's deeper.

So, what to do? What to do if you want to change your reality, but it just feels so... you know... real?

I rely on this simple tool that heightens awareness of when you are falling into those old trenches and awakens a thirst for a new reality.

1) Let your mind go flat. Let it flatten out completely like a totally still lake that stretches out to the horizon.

2) Relax into this calm, flat space and breathe.

3) Think of something you would like in your life. Something that you would like to be part of your new reality.

4) Say these words: "Is it at all within the realm of possibility that _____." (Fill in the blank with the thing you would like to have as part of your new reality.)

5) Go back to your lake. Scan out over that flat, still lake. Imagine you are flying just above the surface of the lake, searching everywhere for this new reality. It doesn't have to be big and fully formed. It can be just the teeny tiniest seed of an idea of what you want.

6) Now, pick up your tiny seed. Cradle it in your hands and gently breathe into it your hopes and dreams. Imagine carefully placing this seed in a little pot of rich dirt. Give it fresh, cool water and lots of sunlight and love. Let it continue to grow as you water it and love it. Feel it becoming stronger and bigger and more fully formed. Transplant it to bigger pots as it grows. Let it be as big as it wants to be.

That is how you create a new reality. What you are doing with this simple and powerful exercise is pulling your mind out of the deep trench of your former "reality," and beginning to dig a new trench for your new "reality" until it is deep enough that you feel more comfortable falling into that one than into the old one.

I have seen clients make amazing transformations in their lives using this one simple tool—shifts that might be called "miracles" because they were profound and there was no logical explanation for them. One client lived in constant, crippling pain. She had a diagnosis of Multiple Sclerosis and had remade her whole life to work within the limited parameters of this reality. As she worked through the emotions of being in so much pain and feeling so limited, she got an image of herself as a fox with its hind leg caught in a big metal trap with sharp teeth. In this image, she felt the sharp teeth cutting into her left leg. She felt the desperation of trying to claw her way free. She sobbed and scrabbled at the big metal trap but could not break loose. She saw herself biting at her leg, gnawing at it with the intention of leaving her foot in the trap and hobbling away on her three remaining legs.

This image, and the feelings that accompanied it, felt so familiar to her. It was all horrible, but it also felt right. As we worked together, she identified many reasons why this feeling felt right to her and cried many cleansing tears. And one day she was ready to do this Simple Meditation. She got into a relaxed state and let her mind go flat. She searched everywhere for just the tiniest seed of true belief that she could live pain-free and whole—that she did not deserve to be in pain or that she must sacrifice her leg to be free. And she found that tiny seed. She picked it up and claimed it. She promised to plant it and water it and give it sunlight. She loved it and helped it grow.

She came back three months later and walked in my door with the proclamation: "I do not have MS anymore!" I grinned and applauded her growing belief. But she said, "No. I'm serious. I got tested and there is no more diagnosis of MS!"

Try it. It's simple. It works. And it can be really fun.

"If you have faith like a grain of mustard seed,
you will say to this mountain,
'Move from here to there,' and it will move.
And nothing will be impossible for you."
Matthew 17:19-20

Notes:

CHAPTER 21

How to Make Peace
With Trauma

I think about trauma a lot. I work with trauma in one of its many guises every day. From one-minute-old babies to 95-year-old grandmothers, it seems no one is exempt. The sad truth is that I feel it in every single person I work with, as well as in myself.

These are the things I have come to know about trauma, now that we are on a first-name basis:

1) Trauma is not selective—it affects anyone and everyone.

2) Trauma is in the eye of the done to, e.g., what might seem like a non-event to one person, is experienced as traumatic by another.

3) No one is doomed to live in a traumatized state. No one is too damaged to heal.

4) These overwhelming events we experience get stuck and mired in our bodies and minds and souls because we have to shut down in the moment just to survive. Those overwhelming events then continue to be stuck in our bodies and trip us up (commonly known as "triggers") because we do not have a fully present, non-judgmental person to help us discharge the trapped, excess energy.

As you move through your day today, notice each person. Imagine what might be motivating them to act the way they are. What possible reason could there by why that woman cut you off and swooped into the parking spot you were waiting for? Why would your son yell how much he hates you and then go straight to his room and slam the door?

When I am at my best, my assumption in every situation, with every person, is that they are doing the very best they can with whatever resources they have at their disposal. We all have battle scars. We all need Grace and Space. This is true of everyone, especially our own selves.

DO THIS:

1) Before reacting to someone today, try to imagine why the other person might be acting that way.

2) Before reacting to yourself today, try to imagine why you might be acting that way.

3) Be a tiny bit kinder to yourself today.

4) If you have a little energy to spare, try to be a little kinder to other people too.

No one is too damaged to heal.

CHAPTER 22

What You Say Is What You Get: Your Words are More Powerful Than You Think

When I work with clients, I am very conscious of their language. Of course, I am aware of their body language, their energy fields, when they look off to the side instead of directly at me, and a whole host of other things like that. But their choice of words is a huge key into what they really believe on an unconscious level.

I have learned that our words work in both directions. They are not just giving voice to our thoughts, they are also shaping and solidifying our thoughts. The act of speaking something out loud actually gives it more power—makes it more real.

This is one of the simplest and most powerful tools I rely upon when working with clients. I simply draw their attention to what they just said, ask them to hear it as they said it, and then rephrase it to more accurately state what they want their reality to be.

One of my clients, a very intelligent forty-five-year-old woman, regularly stated in many different ways that nothing comes easily. "Well, that will take a lot of work to change," "I'll have to think about that and figure out how to work with it," "I'm in this to win this. Anything worth having is worth working hard for." None of those statements is bad. But they do paint a picture of someone who is very committed to a story of always having to work really long and hard for everything she gets.

When I first pointed this pattern out to her, she looked off to the side for a minute and then said, "I've never really thought about it that clearly, but now that you say it, it makes sense." Her whole family, for generations, had been hard-working, blue-collar workers. They took pride in their work ethic and used this as a way to determine inclusion in their family.

I asked her if she wanted to continue always working really hard and long for everything in life. Did she really enjoy the hard work? Or did she want to experience more ease, more flow, more allowing? She said, "I am so tired of always working so incredibly hard for everything I get. I'm exhausted and my body is breaking down from all that I demand of it." She went on to explore the possibility that she could live in a different version of reality where things came to her without so much work. This was a very foreign concept and hard for her to imagine at first. But she played with it, and she began to realize that she could maybe untie some of those strong stories she had been steeped in. She might be able to shift out of some of those stories because she did not want to pass that down to her kids.

She came back several weeks later and said she had been saying a little catch phrase—a little mantra—every time she found herself defaulting to working really hard at something or saying a phrase like the one I had called her out on in my office. Her mantra was, "Everything is easy." As she said each syllable, she touched her thumb to one of her fingers so her body was involved in the rewiring of this generations-old belief. This is so simple. And so brilliant.

Every. Thing. Is. Easy.

Her life today looks very different than it did when we first met. She is a highly successful and well-respected leader in her field who now enjoys her busy and productive life serving others in a way that is fulfilling for her and life-changing for them. She is no longer mired in the heavy sludge of "work for work's sake." She understands now that the prideful hunkering down into "working hard" actually kept her from being the most productive and impactful person she could be.

You can use the power of your words just as effectively as she did.

1) Start noticing things that come out of your mouth regularly. Take note of the patterns.

2) Decide if you like the truth those words communicate.

3) If you do not, start purposefully changing those words to other words that state what you would like your truth to be.

4) Remember that your words shape and solidify your beliefs. Use this to your advantage! Find a little phrase that you can replace that old story with.

5) Catch yourself in the old pattern of thinking and simply replace it with your new phrase. If you can attach it to touching a finger or another physical action, it will be even more powerful.

Notes:

CHAPTER 23

To Receive is Just as Blessed as to Give: Rewriting an Old, Unhealthy Script

I don't know about you, but I am done being told I need to practice more self-care. I am tired of being told to put on my own oxygen mask before I put one on anyone else. I'm sick of seeing memes about filling my own cup so I can pour out into others.

Yes, I know. This is not very PC of me to say. But dang—it's the truth.

The reason I'm sick and tired of it is that it doesn't address the heart of the matter. (And besides, just telling me what to do is not really going to help me much when I need help the most.)

The heart of the matter is this: We are really good at taking care of others, and much better at pouring out than allowing things to pour back in, because when we are flowing outward, we are in control.

When we allow ourselves to soften and receive—when we allow the flow to come inward as well as pour outward—we do not get to call the shots. We don't have control over what will flow back in. We don't have control over how much will flow back in. We don't even have control over when it will flow back in. That can be really scary—especially for those of us who like to keep the reins firmly in our own hands.

But this is the thing: It is not sustainable to always flow outward. It is not even natural. Everything in nature flows in AND out. Everything in nature is set up in cycles and circles—in ebbs and flows.

Were you taught, like me, that it is better to give than to receive? If we live our lives in that way, we are actually moving in an unnatural pattern. We are interrupting the natural flow of energy which must be allowed to flow in at the same velocity and intensity with which it flows out.

1) Notice when you are overly pouring outward.

2) What would it feel like if you were to allow the same velocity and intensity of energy to flow back in that you have poured out?

3) Start paying attention to where you are shutting down the flow of energy that wants to come in.

4) Begin allowing energy to move outward and inward with more ease and comfort—striving to make the energy flowing in equal to the energy flowing out.

This is my prayer for myself, and my hope for you:

Help me be an instrument of thy peace. Help me soften and relax my need to be in control so that I may know the blessing of things flowing in as easily as they flow out.

CHAPTER 24

Ask and You Shall Receive: How to Reverse Engineer Your Life

Related to the idea of "Receiving is as blessed as giving," is the concept of "Ask and you shall receive."

How many times have you heard that phrase?

I've heard it dozens, if not hundreds, of times since I was a little girl in church school. It sounds good, right? The way I always heard it, it seemed so simple: Just ask for something—anything—and BAM! It will be given to you. Sweet! Sign me up!

But what this narrow understanding did over time was undermining and depressing. Because I asked for things, and I didn't get them. I asked and asked...and asked for that sparkly green, three-speed bike with the flower decals and polka-dot seat. I asked so hard! But I didn't get it. I asked for the cash to pay off my credit card debt. But I didn't get it. This story repeated itself over and over and wore my hope and, eventually, my faith down to almost nothing. I assumed my petitions were not right or not powerful enough. Or, even worse, that there was something not right or not powerful enough about ME. That I must not be deserving of receiving what I asked for.

But I have deepened into a broader understanding of this universal truth.

As I meditated on this saying, I began to understand that the two pieces are not actually directly tied to each other. It does not say, "Ask for something and you will get it." It says very clearly only two things:

1) Ask.

 and

2) Receive.

Isn't that interesting. We make this assumption—we build a mental bridge between the two parts. But they were never actually tied to each other at all.

What this is really saying is that we must be living, breathing invitations. We are not equations: We are not X and that equals Y. We must open ourselves to being an invitation to the universal flow—that soul-filling coming and going—that circular fulfillment (see Chapter 23).

When we are not fighting this flow by throwing up roadblocks of guilt and unworthiness, making things more difficult and complicated than they need to be, or by trying to control what is not ours to control—then we are free to simply surrender into the universal stream and watch everything come and go with perfect ease.

Ask.

Receive.

As I have worked with this phrase, I have seen powerful changes in my life. I would love for you to experience this power in your own life.

1) Put yourself into an open, prayerful "Asking Space." In this space, you are totally humble and open-hearted. You are acknowledging that you are not the boss of everything and that you need some loving assistance from a greater source than yourself.

2) Now, put yourself into an open, prayerful "Receiving Space." In this space, you are totally unstructured and curious. You are acknowledging that you are not the boss of everything and that you are willing to let things flow in that are not in your control.

3) Watch carefully and note ALL the ways you receive. Write them all down.

4) Offer a prayer of gratitude for ALL you receive—whether these things seem specifically related to your prayer or not.

That open, prayerful space—that "Receiving Space"—allows things to flow into your life in unexpected ways. These things may or may not seem to have anything to do with what you were specifically asking for. But all of them are actually exactly what you asked for and what will most lovingly help you on a deep, soul level.

Pro Tip: You can reverse engineer this practice. Everything in our lives is an answer to conscious or unconscious prayers. Remember that prayers can just be things we spend a lot of time thinking and worrying about. My Grandma Kay always said, "Worries are just prayers you don't want answered."

Let's say you don't like the fact that every time you pay off the last of your debt, something happens that puts you right back in debt again. What prayer could you be praying that would look like this if it was going to be answered? Obvious worries/prayers would be something like: Life is difficult. You have to work hard to get ahead. You are a sinner, and sinners don't deserve to be debt-free and happy. If things go too well, you better watch for that other foot to fall. It is easier for a camel to go through the eye of a needle, than a rich person to get into heaven (e.g., you better make sure you are never mistaken for a rich person), etc.

Now, the most important step—the step where you fine-tune and really hone-in on working in divine synchronicity: Really notice what you receive. Notice all of it. Ask yourself this: What parts of what I am receiving do I love? And what was I likely asking for (both consciously and unconsciously) that these parts I love would be an answer to? And what parts of what I am receiving do I not like? And what is the most likely thing I'm asking for (both consciously and unconsciously) that these parts I don't love would be an answer to?

Once you have some ideas about these things, you can more quickly and fully notice when you are thinking things that are going to bring in more of what you don't want, and start to shift that thinking to something that will bring in more of what you do want!

Just as you cannot inhale without exhaling,
you can't receive without asking.
What are you asking for?

1) Look at your life and ask yourself, "What prayers am I praying on an unconscious level that are being answered to create THIS?"

2) Figure that out.

3) Now, start purposefully replacing those prayers that you think are resulting in the things you don't like, with more conscious prayers for the things you do want.

4) Be very purposeful. Get better and better at catching yourself worrying/praying for what you don't want and replace that with asking for/praying for what you do want.

Notes:

CHAPTER 25

The Power Hidden in Just Breathing

Throughout this book, we have been settling into the idea that we do not have to make massive changes to experience profound results. We have explored many small positive things we can do in our day-to-day lives—things that do not require expensive equipment or a graduate degree to effectively implement. Each of these small things is powerful in its own right and worthy of your time and attention. But there is one small tool that we have not looked at—one tool that is always with you, that is so ubiquitous it is usually taken for granted, and one that requires only a moment of attention to experience its full power: That tool is your breath.

Think about how often you feel separate and alone—isolated, even cut off. This feeling begins at birth. Before birth, our every need is met fully and effortlessly—our sustenance flows into our bodies through no effort of our own, our body temperature is maintained perfectly, we continue to grow with divine determinism, there is no concept of "separate" or even "other."

This state of bliss is rudely interrupted when we are born into light and noise and smells and direct touch. Our lungs are immediately filled with strong air rather than gentle water. We must instantly learn to breathe in order to survive—we are suddenly required to be an active participant in our own lives.

This active participation soon becomes second nature. We are not required to think about breathing in order to move air in and out of our lungs and keep ourselves alive. But it is interesting to note that breathing is the only action of the human body that is both autonomic (does not require thought) and somatic (requires thought).

We can use this truth to our advantage. While it is true our breathing is autonomic, it is also highly reactionary: When we are nervous or frightened, worried or feeling unsafe, our breath becomes sporadic and shallow. This forms a negative feedback loop in our systems whereby we are now in fight-or-flight so our breathing reflects that—but our sporadic, shallow breathing also reinforces for our bodies that we are correct to stay in fight-or-flight.

The quickest way cut of this all-too-common negative feedback loop is to consciously take a deep breath. Or two. Or three. Each diaphragmatic breath you take—deep down into your belly—tells your body that there is no imminent threat. You activate your parasympathetic nervous system which pumps out all of the feel-good hormones and helps you down-regulate into a resting and comfortable state.

Other mammals use this tool regularly. If you have a dog, you will notice that when it is stressed, it yawns. When it is trying to calm down, it will even seek out your eye contact and give a big yawn. Dog trainers teach that if you yawn back at it, you are communicating that, "All is well. No need to be on high alert. It is okay for you to be at ease."

We can do the same thing for our own systems. Many studies have shown that we change our bodies on a cellular level when we slow our breathing. A systematic review of fifteen gold-standard studies published in 2018 in Frontiers of Human Neuroscience, concluded that slow breathing is related to "...increased comfort, relaxation, pleasantness, vigor and alertness, and reduced symptoms of arousal, anxiety, depression, anger, and confusion" (Zaccaro, et al. How Breath-Control Can Change Your Life: A Systematic Review on Psycho-Physiological Correlates of Slow Breathing).

Many practices around the world teach specific breathing techniques for this very reason: Pregnant people take classes on how to breathe in labor to stay calmer and more focused as well as harness the happy hormones that are released when they do; athletes are trained to use their breath to increase performance; ancient Indian, Chinese and Japanese breath practices have been passed down for centuries as tools for enjoying a more grounded and fulfilling life.

It is also interesting that the root word for "breath" in Ancient Greek is "pneuma" which translates as "spirit." In Old Hebrew, the word for "breath" is "ruach" which is translated interchangeably as "spirit" and "essential nature."

Knowing that the etymology of the word "breath" is the same in multiple languages makes this even more resonant. Understanding that people in many cultures and over many lifetimes have experienced this truth has changed my relationship with my own breathing. I am more aware that I am quite literally bringing spirit into my innermost self every time I breathe. I close my eyes and I feel the intrinsic power of breath—of spirit—filling and invigorating life into every corner of my being.

We pray by breathing.
- Thomas Merton

1. Begin to notice your own breath throughout the day. How deep is it? How fast is it? What does it do when you interact with certain people? What happens to your breath when you need to have a difficult conversation or find yourself in a confrontation with your children? What does it do when you are doing something normal like washing the dishes or driving to work?

2. Catch yourself in unconscious moments. Notice your breath and purposefully slow and deepen it. Notice where in your body you feel your breath stopping—does it flow in effortlessly clear down into your belly? Or does it stop in your throat or your chest? Try to deepen it.

3. Imagine that your breath is filled with spirit—actually is spirit. Feel the power of breathing in spirit and allowing it to infuse every cell in your body.

4. Take a cue from your dog and give a big yawn if you can't get your breath to slow and deepen any other way.

If you want to go even deeper, you can look into taking some classes on breathwork or working with a private instructor. There are many practitioners and teachers who teach pranayama and other breathing techniques that will help you unleash the full power of this simple tool. Just look up "breathing classes" in your area for a listing of options.

CONCLUSION

"Beyond a wholesome discipline,
be gentle with yourself.

You are a child of the universe, no less than
the trees and the stars.

You have a right to be here. And whether or
not it is clear to you, no doubt the universe is
unfolding as it should."

– Max Ehrmann

CONCLUSION

As I finish writing this book, my heart is full of hope. Hope that you will remember the tools in this book when you are going about your normal day. Hope that you have found some little ways to help you more easily navigate difficult situations. Hope that you experience profound results from applying these simple tools.

But more than all that, hope you know that I believe in you. I believe that anything—let me say that again—anything is possible for you. I believe that you are a good person who is getting even better. You have proven this to me, and to yourself, simply by picking up this book. I believe you are smart enough, motivated enough, love-filled enough, and brave enough to dive head-first into the challenging and joyful process of using these little tools to become the biggest, boldest, most beautiful expression of exactly who you are.

Get busy. The world needs more of you.

www.ingramcontent.com/pod-product-compliance
Lightning Source LLC
LaVergne TN
LVHW050045090426
835510LV00043B/3026